*ESSENTIAL
CHAN BUDDHISM*

ESSENTIAL CHAN BUDDHISM

The Character and Spirit of Chinese Zen

CHAN MASTER GUO JUN

FOREWORD BY ROBERT A. F. "TENZIN" THURMAN

Monkfish Book Publishing Company
Rhinebeck, New York

ESSENTIAL CHAN BUDDHISM
The Character and Spirit of Chinese Zen
© 2013, 2024 Chan Master Guo Jun

Paperback ISBN 978-1-958972-18-2
eBook ISBN 978-1-939681-03-4

Library of Congress Cataloging-in-Publication Data

Names: Guo, Jun, 1974- author.
Title: Essential Chan Buddhism : the character and spirit of Chinese Zen /
    Chan Master Guo Jun.
Description: Rhinebeck : Monkfish Book Publishing Company, 2024.
Identifiers: LCCN 2023007499 | ISBN 9781958972182 (paperback)
Subjects: LCSH: Spiritual life–Zen Buddhism. | Zen Buddhism--Doctrines.
Classification: LCC BQ9288 .G86 2024 | DDC 294.3/444--dc23/eng/20230222
LC record available at https://lccn.loc.gov/2023007499

Calligraphy by Master Sheng Yen and Master Guo Jun
Cover design by Colin Rolfe

Monkfish Book Publishing Company
22 E. Market St., Suite 304
Rhinebeck, NY 12572
(845) 876-4861
monkfishpublishing.com

Foreword

It is my pleasure and privilege to introduce Chan Master Guo Jun to English-language readers. Guo Jun is Chinese but was born in Singapore and raised in centers of Chan teaching and practice in Korea as well as China. He was also trained as a hard scientist, and he seems to fully understand Chan as primarily a Buddhist mind science with heavy-duty inner lab work, and not just religion. He is the youngest dharma heir to Master Sheng Yen, one of the most renowned and accomplished Buddhist teachers of the late twentieth century, who passed on in 2009.

I was very fond of Master Sheng Yen, and I like to think that he was fond of me. We met in the 1990s when I arranged for him to co-teach with His Holiness the Dalai Lama. Our little Tibet House US rented Roseland, the famous jazz club in New York, and invited the two dharma masters. After much preparatory work, they met at the appointed time, dialogued with each other, and taught a large audience about the Transcendent Wisdom Heart Sutra, each in his own way. They enjoyed each other, enjoyed the sutra and its teaching of insight of the universal compassion bodhisattva, Avalokitesvara, about emptiness, and gave something very profound to the ethnically very diverse American audience. We took delight in the fact that in a jazz club many fans who were "real gone" out of their skulls over Charlie Parker riffs got to celebrate a different version of the great wisdom mantra, "gone, gone, very gone, very totally gone beyond—all hail enlightenment!"

Later, Master Sheng Yen supported Buddhist Studies at Columbia University from his foundation, endowing a professorship. I wasn't the one who asked him to do that, but I was very happy that he extended his gracious teachings in that way, reaching out to future generations of students to let them know something about the great traditions of Buddhist thought and practice from India, China, and Tibet, without asking anyone to be a "Buddhist." Master Sheng Yen had the real enlightenment to know that human beings have a lot to learn, and that learning is essential to the path of being a good human being, and maybe even finding some sort of enlightenment for life, something that is far beyond mere religious belief. When the inaugural ceremony was arranged, I was told that the master requested that I be present, which I was looking forward to doing. Sadly, he became too ill to visit New York at the time, and to my regret, he passed away before I was able to meet him again. But as Master Guo Jun says in this precious little book, our kind teachers are with us all the time, present or not, and they teach us wherever and whenever we are open to learn.

From reading his book, I find Master Guo Jun, though I do not yet know him personally and of course I have only a very limited perspective, carries on Master Sheng Yen's legacy with great nobility and good-humored eloquence. The book gives sound teachings, documenting Master Guo Jun's rigorous training, perseverance in austere retreats from which others fled, long hours in meditation, numberless prostrations, hard-won wisdom, and absolute commitment to Chan, the Chinese form of Zen.

In our era where China is known for its wholesale adoption of Western materialism, its booming economy and environmental self-destruction, its government's oppression of its own people, and its colonialist annexations, occupations, and exploitations of Mongolia, Turkestan, and Tibet, it is very good to read a book that brings us back to the essence of the Chinese heart, to sense the realistic intelligence of one of the primary strands of Chinese Buddhist spirituality. It gives us hope, by putting us back in touch with the compassionate and contemplative side of the Chinese character and spirit.

Chan is not at all as well known in the West as Zen, but it is the child of the great adept traditions of India and the parent of Korean Son and

Japanese Zen. It has flourished and continued its development through many great masters, on a parallel track with Son and Zen for much of the last millennia. In essence, these Chan, Son, Zen, and Vietnamese Thien traditions are fully on the same wavelength and depth, but each also has its own flavor, texture, and inflection in the way it delivers wisdom to its admirers and practitioners. As it enters into our Western melting-pot cultures, we need the diverse approaches and gifts of all the great lineages of the tradition.

In this highly readable book, Master Guo Jun brings Chan's profound and powerful teachings to the page in a form is that is accessible, poetic, spontaneous, and full of warmth, humor, and deep insight. As I read, I was thrilled by his respect for learning as indispensable for the fruitful path, the unlearned practitioner being like an empty cup, and his clear explanation of the three further flaws of the cup (being dirty or poisoned, being covered or inverted, and being cracked and leaky, representing the wrongly motivated, the proud, and the forgetful learners). I loved his lucid description of the practice of prostration, so important for life and spiritual growth. And of course I am always inspired by a central theme of his, of loving the breath, of cherishing the moment to moment thread of vital existence discoverable by constant returning, again and again, and how he connects that to the special Chinese science and wisdom of the *chi*, the vital energy also explored with enormous sophistication by the Tantric adepts of India and Tibet. I was fully won over especially by the following passage that has to have emerged from his own deep experience:

Sitting itself will not give you enlightenment. Meditation will not give it to you. It will only lead you to the brink. Retreating from the world will not liberate you. Happiness is not found in a secluded forest hut or an isolated cave. Enlightenment comes when you connect to the world. Only when you truly connect with everyone and everything else do you become enlightened. Only by going deeply and fully into the world do you attain liberation. This is the meaning of the star—the sudden illumination of our connection to the rest of the universe.

He refers here to the morning star that Shakyamuni is said to have perceived at the predawn twilight of his supreme enlightenment. I love the nondualism of his insight, which so strongly counters the tendency of Buddhists to think of Nirvana as a departure from the world, an absolute transcendence that goes into a place of total quiescence that awaits beyond the world. Too many practitioners imagine such as the goal to seek, not thinking critically about the selfish "oneness" of such an obliterative "freedom." I believe the Chan expression here is that entering such a state through meditative self-absorption is to fall into entrapment in "the demon ghost cave." But our author, Master Guo Jun, here is very clear that Nirvana is the fullest embrace of the world, recognizing Nirvana as nondually one with the world in all its richness of detail, fullness of self and others, and therefore the only thing left as an absolute is just natural compassion for anyone who suffers by misknowing their true reality.

I very much admire and enjoy this book, and I am honored to introduce it. It is a window into the heart and soul of China, as its great people will once again rise above their materialist obsessions and regain the splendor of their inheritance of spiritual greatness handed on to them by their world treasure dharma masters. This book of the teachings of Master Guo Jun is to be treasured, not only by Buddhists, but also by serious humanists and spiritual seekers of all kinds.

Robert A. F. "Tenzin" Thurman

Jey Tsong Khapa Professor of Buddhist Studies,
Columbia University

Author of *Infinite Life* and other works

Editor's Note

I HOPE THIS book captures the flavor and incantatory style of Guo Jun's spoken English in the talks he gave at a fourteen-day retreat at Chan Forest in the hills outside Jakarta in 2010 and in the subsequent conversations we had there during the winter of 2011.

I have tried to do justice to the complexity of Guo Jun's character and the beauty and rigor of his teachings. Chan is not as well known in the West as Zen, Tibetan, or some forms of Theravada Buddhism. I hope this book will help, at least a little bit, to remedy that.

I wanted to show in the text how Chan is part of Chinese, not just Buddhist, culture. Guo Jun grew up in Singapore as part of a Chinese family, and the ways in which he is self-consciously Chinese are clear and considered, more so, perhaps, than if he had grown up on the mainland or Taiwan.

My wife, Corinne Mol, who has extensive practice in various meditation traditions including Chan, carefully sifted through and glossed the retreat talks and organized them. Together we developed the book's table of contents to represent the essence of Guo Jun's teaching to his Indonesian students.

My thanks to Agus Santoso for getting this off the ground and to the Tigris brothers, Buntario and Selamat, for their wonderful hospitality. And to Ibu Kiki, who taught me my first few words in Indonesian and introduced me to Indonesia's many luscious fruits!

Kenneth Wapner

Woodstock, New York
2013

1

Impermanence

How long is your life?

One day, the Buddha asked his disciples: "How long is life?"

"Maybe fifty years?" replied a disciple.

"Wrong," said Buddha.

Another disciple said, "Months."

"No," Buddha said.

"Days? Weeks?" another disciple suggested.

"Wrong. Wrong," said Buddha. "Not years, not months, not weeks, not days."

Then they asked: "How long is our life?"

"Our life is only as long as one breath."

2

Tigers and Pussycats

I STARTED LEARNING Buddhism in 1987, when I was fourteen years old. I went on my first seven-day Chan retreat at seventeen. I did other retreats of varying lengths when I was in my teens and early twenties. My parents were simple people, expatriate Chinese living in Singapore. I was training to be a genetic engineer, but Buddhism called to me.

My head was shaved by Master Song Nian at Singapore's Mahabodhi Monastery on Easter day in 1997. I did sutra studies at Taiwan's Buddhist Institute. After that, I wanted to experience different forms of Chan practice and I wanted to test myself. So in 1999 and 2000 I went on three-month intensive summer and winter retreats at Korean Son monasteries in Seoul and Gwangju. Son, the Korean form of Chan or Zen, had a reputation for being very rigorous. That was what I wanted, and I was not disappointed.

The daily schedule was brutal. We woke at 3:00 AM and finished at 11:00 PM. We had only fifteen minutes each for breakfast, lunch, and dinner. Toilet breaks were five minutes, but the toilet was far from the meditation hall. We had no time, so we just went outside to shoot. For ninety days we did not take a shower. We had a basin of water that was filled from a bamboo pipe that ran down from the mountain and used a towel to scrub ourselves clean.

No break time, no time to relax, no nap after lunch. Sleeping after 11:00. Waking at 3:00. Most of us did not even have a room. We sat in the meditation hall on a folded-up cushions, which were also our beds. Each sitting was at least an hour, and we had to sit in full lotus. No movement was tolerated. If the monitors, who were senior monks, saw us move an inch, they'd hit us with the incense stick. In the morning, after waking, we had to do 108 prostrations in only ten minutes. Up and down, up and down. It looked like we were doing jumping jacks.

The Korean terminology for this kind of intensive retreat is *Kyol Che*, which means "very tight dharma." You have to be very fast, very precise, always in the moment. There is no time to think, wander off, and daydream. If you fall behind, you get hit. There is nothing symbolic about these blows. *Thwack!* You dare not whimper or cringe. They punch and kick you, and you have to bow and gently say, "thank you." In Korean.

And then there is pain, so much pain. Tears roll

down from your eyes the moment you move your legs as you come out of the full lotus. There is so much pain that you don't know where the pain is coming from. You try to massage your muscles, but it's not the muscles. The pain goes into the bone. At the end of the day you are so tired you cannot move or stand up. You crawl to bed.

And then the food. Kimchi all the time, kimchi and white rice. The kimchi smelled like rotten eggs. It was repulsive, almost unbearable. It made me gag, and I had to force down every bite. It was the only food, so you either ate it or starved! A piece of tofu was an extravagance. We ate tofu three or four times in ninety days. The rest of the time it was kimchi with black beans and a few sprouts.

For seven days and nights in the middle of the retreat we were subjected to what is called in Chinese *yong men jin jing*, which translates as "great courageous diligence." This was an even more intensive practice than your run-of-the-mill *Kyol Che*. For seven days and nights we were not allowed to lie down. Twenty-four hours of continuous sitting practice for seven straight days. We learned how to sleep while sitting, but when you were caught dozing, you were hit. You learned to sleep without moving.

Before going into the Son retreat they warned us that it was called the demon training camp. We called it the cave of the tiger.

Once you enter the cave of the tiger you can only come out in two ways. One, you die. If it's summer, they will carry your corpse out of the *Son Bang*, the Chan Hall. But if you die in the winter, they put you under the table. It is so cold in the unheated hall that your body will not rot. Then they take you out for burial after the retreat is over.

The second way to leave *Son Bang* is to be verified that you are enlightened. Then you can walk away before the retreat ends.

Those are the two acceptable ways to leave the retreat. But sometimes, in the ninety days, the person next to you would disappear. They had escaped. In the middle of night, they had climbed over the monastery's wall and run away. When that happened their name was published and the whole of Korea knew they had run. For the next three years, that person was blacklisted—banned from the Chan Hall and Chan monasteries in all of Korea.

I WENT ON the retreat with one of my friends, a Chinese monk from Malaysia. We had received the precepts together.

"Are you sure you want to go to the retreat?" I asked him before we traveled to Korea.

"Yes, I'm sure," he replied.

"Have you settled everything?"

"Yes."

"For ninety days you have to practice. It's very serious. These are very extreme practices."

"No problem."

So we went on the retreat together.

On the third day, he pulled my shirt.

"What?" I asked.

"I want to go home."

"Why?"

"I forgot some things I have to do in Malaysia."

"Didn't I tell you to plan and settle everything beforehand? Why didn't you plan properly?"

"I forgot. I have to go home."

"Try to endure," I said.

The next day he said he had heart pain and his nose was beginning to bleed. We went to see the head monk, an older man, after everyone went to bed. His quarters were very simple, very basic. We exchanged formalities, bows, and prostrations to each other.

"What do you want?" he asked with stern and staring eyes.

"I have to leave because I forgot—" my friend began.

The head monk immediately interrupted. "I understand," he replied. "All the best." He dismissed us, and my friend was released.

After my friend left the Koreans laughed at us Chinese. They said that nowadays Chinese monks cannot practice, meditate, or endure hardship. They looked down on us Chinese and said Chinese Buddhism was finished. "In China, people don't practice," they said. "They're all like pussycats. The pussycat has come into the tiger cave and become frightened and run away."

I was unhappy. I felt I had to show the Koreans that this Chinese can take hardship. But throughout the retreat I thought of giving up and going home from the moment I woke up until I went to sleep.

How did I sustain myself? I kept coming back to the present moment, kept coming back to the present moment, kept coming back to the present moment. I learned to relax. There were six Chinese monks who went into the cave of the tiger. At the end of the retreat, I was the only one left. I completed the retreat and went for a second and a third. Altogether, 270 days.

WE CHINESE WERE not the only ones who bolted. A retreat usually started with fifty to sixty Korean monks and by the end there were maybe thirty left. In Korea, they have a lot of respect for monks from the *Son Bang*. They are called *yi deng he shang*, top class, grade-one monk. When the big monasteries select an abbot, they choose one from the *Son Bang*.

At this point in my life I was young and my health was better than it is today. I didn't want to lose face, so I stuck it out. The retreats took their toll, however. In winter, Korea has a Siberian climate. It was freezing in the unheated Chan Hall. I was quite young, a junior monk, so I couldn't afford winter clothing. I wore ten T-shirts, each on top of the other. No matter how many T-shirts I wore it wasn't enough. There were no blankets for sleeping. I curled up, a shivering mess, on my thin cushion. After the retreat, my health was affected, and I coughed for five years.

This type of retreat may not have been healthy for the body, but it tested the will to practice. The retreats trained my perseverance, or as we say, *dao xin*—my "mind for the path."

I returned to Korea nine years later to find that this type of retreat is not so common anymore. It is being lost. In any case, now that I'm in my late thirties, I don't think I could withstand this type of the training. *Kyol Che* is for the young and healthy, and I think if I were to try it again, this pussycat would probably end up dead and frozen under the table in the Chan Hall.

3

Breath

In Chan, you fall in love with your breath.

You think about the breath while you're sitting, eating, and walking. After you finish your work, you think about the breath. The breath comes to your mind. You want to get close to the breath. There is a tenderness, sweetness, and intimacy that you want to share with the breath. You want to give your time to the breath; you want to give your whole self to the breath. You want to take care of the breath. The breath is very precious, just as the person you love is precious. You treat the breath with gentleness and care.

When you cannot find the breath, you don't get angry, in the same way that when you cannot find the person you love, you don't get angry; you just keep thinking: Where is she? Similarly, the breath, being your most loyal and loved one, will not desert you. It will not stop searching or looking for you when you are lost. It will find you; all you need to do is just be still, and it will come to you by your side.

Give yourself to the breath as if you are giving to the person you love. Give it your life. Your everything. Have this kind of intimacy, longing, and fondness for the breath. Forgive the breath when it becomes short and rough. Do not rise up in anger against it. Accept the breath as it is. Love and accept it.

Falling in love gives you energy. It is the same when you fall in love with your breath. You think about the breath when you wake up. You are enthusiastic. You have energy.

Falling in love with your breath is called the meditation of love. People sometimes think that in Buddhism love is something that is frowned upon and relationships are no good. This is because relationships necessarily involve attachment and grasping, and Buddhism often teaches us to detach. We should let go of intimate relationships because they are a constant struggle, and struggle is, inevitably, a source of suffering.

Chan teaches us to love with no attachment. To care without imposing. To love in the way we love the breath.

THE BREATH IS always there. It never leaves us. We abandon our breath, run away from our breath, ignore the breath. The breath is always there, waiting for us. The breath is always there, precisely as the present moment is always here.

We are born with the most precious thing there is, which money cannot buy. We are born with the breath. From the moment we are born until the moment we die, our most loyal friend is the breath. It stays with us. And yet, so often, we neglect this friend and take it for granted. We ignore the breath. We betray the breath. But when we want to go back to the breath, the breath welcomes us.

The breath is our treasure. It gives us courage and support. The breath is our refuge. Keep returning and returning and returning to the breath.

Perhaps this sounds easy. It is not. Nothing that is precious and to be cherished is easy. If you can get it easily, it is not precious.

It is not easy to always come back to the breath, to come back to the present moment. Still, in reality, it is quite simple. We are born with the breath; we are born with Buddha nature. At the end of the day, it is our choice. We all have a choice to follow the path back to the breath and the present moment. It is a matter of whether we want to do it or not.

Fall in love with the breath, with coming back to the present moment. Treat the breath like your closest friend, the person you want share your deepest self with, from whom there are no secrets, with whom you want to share all your joys and sorrows. Treat the breath like your closest friend, a friend you want to make part of your life.

4

Heart-to-Heart:
Sitting

In Chan, we sit in meditation, always coming back to the breath, coming back to the present moment.

Why is sitting "the practice" of Chan? Why is it so fundamental? Where does it come from? Is it our practice because Buddha sat under the Bodhi Tree when he became enlightened? Or because, legend has it, Bodhidharma, the first Chan patriarch, sat in front of a blank wall for nine years?

Perhaps. But I would like to talk about sitting and Chan from another angle.

Sitting is a part of our daily lives. We take a rest by sitting. We sit to eat, draw, write, and talk with friends. When we share good things, we sit. You don't really have a good chat with someone when you are standing up or walking. When you want to talk heart-to-heart, you sit. Sitting brings people closer together.

Sitting is a foundation. It's part of our development, both as individuals and as a species. The child must

12

learn to sit before he can stand up. We distinguish ourselves from animals because we stand upright. Animals crawl. Sitting is the transition between animals and humans.

With sitting, we are able to concentrate for long periods. It is our creative posture, our posture of concentration and absorption in the work of the mind and dexterous tasks. It is said we evolved as humans when we were able to stand upright and use our hands. But think of how much we owe to the person who sits, absorbed in his or her task!

When we are sad, we keep to ourselves. But we also sit. Sitting is a way to recover, to gradually let what is inside us resolve. It creates stability. There is a sense of grounding when we sit. Sitting is a way to give ourselves comfort.

I FELT SOME of this when I first started sitting on the small island of Pulau Ubin outside Singapore. I went on retreat as a teenager in a very small Buddhist center. The experience of sitting deepened for me in the mountains of Malaysia outside Penang. I felt myself coming back to my body. I felt myself coming home.

These early sitting experiences were interwoven with the feeling of being close to nature. The retreats took place in a lush mountain jungle or near the ocean. As I sat, I listened to the aliveness of the forest and waves lapping rhythmically against the shore.

My parents were concerned with what was happening to me. They were very simple people, involved in Chinese folk beliefs. They worshipped many gods and our ancestors.

I had the fire of Chan in me, and I was often away. But my schoolwork and character improved as I took to the Buddhist path. They could not find fault. I had been a lackadaisical, rebellious child. My character reformed and they were pleased. But they missed me.

The feeling of coming home when I first started sitting was a coming back to something that was already there. Chan is going back to what we already have and know. It is going back to our original nature. What is that? Sitting. We know how to do it. Chan is a rediscovery of what we already have.

When we sit, we come back to ourselves.

When we finish thinking, we stand up.

When we want to say sorry from our hearts, we sit.

After that we stand and embrace.

And continue on the path.

This is my understanding of sitting.

5

RELAXATION

To RELAX IS the beginning of Chan. To relax your body and mind. Relaxation is the goal and the main purpose of Chan practice. Please do not misunderstand me. To be relaxed is not to be lazy. To be relaxed simply means there is no tension, stress, or pressure.

THERE IS A Chinese story about a man, a retiree, who went fishing. A young man sat down next to him and was also fishing.

"Hey, young man. What are you doing here?" the old man said.

"Same as you," the young man replied.

"Really!" said the old man. "I'm enjoying myself. I'm relaxing! I've finished school. I've finished my career and raising my children. They have grown up and become independent. I am finished with all the responsibilities of my life. As a result, now I can relax and enjoy myself."

The young man laughed. "I'm also enjoying myself.

I'm also relaxed."

"Are you?" said the old man. "I don't think so."

This story points to the true nature of relaxation. In order to truly relax, you need to work hard and fulfill your responsibilities. After the young man has finished fishing, he has to go back to his life. Perhaps he has to look for a job, go to school, or return to his family. He still has problems. But the old man? There is nothing he needs to worry about. This is what the Chan Master Zhaozhou Congshen (778–897) meant when he said: "When I'm hungry I eat; when I'm thirsty I drink; when I'm tired I sleep."

So easy, we think: I know how to eat, drink, and sleep. It is true that relaxation may appear to be simple. But it is not necessarily easy. How do we relax? By coming back to the breath. By coming back to the present moment. Stop brooding over the past and worrying about the future. The past is gone and the future is always unknown and uncertain. Breathe. One breath at a time. Relax.

To relax means to be receptive. If you are able to relax, you will absorb things easily and your memory will be sharp and clear.

As you relax, you develop tolerance and endurance and enlarge the capacity of your heart and mind. You open up. You are able to receive more. Relaxation creates space. You become more accommodating. You no longer feel cramped and tight. A small heart has no room. Buddha heart is as big as the universe. Limitless.

By learning how to relax, we increase our ability to take pain and cushion ourselves against the inevitable problems and suffering that comes from living.

Painful emotions and thoughts are like naughty, mischievous children. They pull your shirt, climb all over you, tug your ears, and beat on you with their little fists. The more you shoo them away, the more they pester you. When you don't react and just relax, after a short time they see that you are no fun and let you be.

When you react, the emotion says, "Great! He wants to play with me. Let's play together." So the emotion comes back for more.

Each time you relax, the energy or strength of what's bothering you will weaken. In Chinese Buddhism, we have the image of Maitreya, the fat, smiling, happy Buddha. Children sit on his head and shoulders and crawl all over him. And the Buddha is still laughing because he is very friendly and relaxed.

With any weighty problem, our tendency is to chew it with our minds, looking for a solution. Our minds probe, search, analyze, and run here and there. We think that when we relax we're not being proactive or productive. But this is not necessarily the case. Thinking crowds the mind. It becomes like a sky full of clouds. As a result, the sun cannot shine. There is no brightness or light.

If you clear up your mind, you may actually make a discovery and find something you've missed. Or you may be able to see what has been troubling you from a different perspective. All great scientific discoveries came when they were least expected. Suddenly, out of the blue, a solution appeared!

Relax, calm down, clear the mind, breathe, come back into the present moment. Then you are able to see a way through. When you relax, everything becomes clear. Your senses sharpen and your mind becomes bright.

6

Connecting to
the World

Perhaps it is only a legend, but I like the story
of Buddha attaining enlightenment when he saw a
shooting star, recounted in the early Buddhist text,
the *Transmission of the Lamp*. It's very Chan—the
sudden illumination blazing across the sky in a
brilliant, breathtaking flash. Then gone.

Sitting itself will not give you enlightenment.
Meditation will not give it to you. It will only lead
you to the brink. Retreating from the world will not
liberate you. Happiness is not found in a secluded
forest hut or an isolated cave. Enlightenment
comes when you connect to the world. Only when
you truly connect with everyone and everything
else do you become enlightened. Only by going
deeply and fully into the world do you attain
liberation. This is the meaning of the star—the
sudden illumination of our connection to the rest
of the universe.

7

FARMING MEDITATION

WHEN BUDDHISM SPREAD from India to China, it needed time to adapt and adjust itself. The teachings didn't change but they assimilated certain aspects of Chinese culture. Chan is very much a product of both Chinese culture and Buddhism.

The early history of Buddhism in China is complex and shrouded in legend. Buddhism was probably first introduced in China about two thousand years ago during the Han dynasty and bumped up against the already-established religions of Confucianism and Taoism. It resonated with certain aspects of Taoism. Early Sanskrit Buddhist texts that were translated into Chinese have a certain Taoist flavor.

According to tradition, the White Horse Temple was established in 68 CE in Henan Province. It is said to be the cradle of Chinese Buddhism. Buddhism took hold and grew. Then, in 446, Emperor Taiwu sought to suppress it, destroying monasteries, Buddhist art and texts, and killing monks.

When Taiwu died, his successor, Emperor Wencheng, restored Buddhism. There were a number of different Buddhist schools, including the Pure Land and Tiantai (which emphasized the Lotus Sutra). Tradition has the Indian sage Bodhidharma arriving in China in about 500 CE. Bodhidharma sat in front of a blank wall for nine years. So Chan was born.

Buddhism took on a distinctly Chinese character when it came to China. During the time of the Buddha and for hundreds of years afterward in India, monastics—both monks and nuns—lived a wandering life in the warm forests, collecting alms for their food. This kind of renunciative wandering life was already established in India, and, in fact, it was how Buddha lived both before and after enlightenment.

The first Buddhists were nomadic ascetics. In exchange for alms, they would teach, sharing their wisdom, which had a tangible value in the society in which they lived. That tradition continues in India today. Wandering *sadhus* crisscross the land with alms bowls and staffs and little else. It is a hard life of freedom and beauty, but in China it never worked for a variety of reasons. For one thing, in most parts of China during much of the year, if you slept in the forest in simple robes you would freeze.

More importantly, there were cultural reasons that asceticism didn't take hold in China. Not only would you freeze in China if you wandered around collecting alms, you would probably starve. In China, beggars, even those with august religious traditions behind them, are despised. Confucius had taught that you should give back to your family and society. He stressed industriousness—a strong work ethic. His was a philosophy of the here and now, of how to make our day-to-day life run smoothly and efficiently.

Buddhism changed in China with the establishment of monasteries that supported themselves through agriculture. The first Chan monastery was built by Mazu Daoyi (709–88) at Kung-kung Mountain in southern Kiangsi Province. He had many disciples and is credited as the most influential teacher in the history of Chan.

With the advent of Chan monasteries, the lifestyle of Chinese Buddhists changed. Legend has it that Master Baizhang set down rules for the monastic discipline and formalized this new kind of life: monastics would farm and support themselves instead of begging for food. Baizhang famously said: "One day without work is one day without food."

The establishment of monasteries was not only a result of adopting a Chinese work ethic.

Monasteries in China were large, sometimes containing thousands of people. If these large numbers of monks went into villages to beg, it would have been like robbing the village. How could the villagers, who usually had only enough for themselves, supply so much food?

Also at this time, the diets of monks changed. They became vegetarians. This was in line with the Mahayana vow of great compassion, or *bodhicitta*. If we look into the teaching of no-self, we know that all sentient beings are interrelated. We see ourselves in all sentient beings.

Indian Buddhists had not been vegetarians. When you're begging for alms, you take what you can get, meat included. Some Mahayana traditions retain the practice of eating meat, but that is largely because, in Tibet at least, there is little arable land and the nomadic life of herders is tied to yaks. Tibetan Buddhists don't feast on meat.

During the early period of Chinese Buddhism, we see what's called *nong chan* in Chinese. *Nong* means "hoe," "cultivation," "farmer," and "farming." *Nong chan* is farming meditation, which ties Chan into the very roots of Chinese agrarian society. It is not surprising—although it is somewhat ironic— that the refined language of Chinese philosophical discourse is steeped in the agrarian tradition; after all, the farmers were illiterate peasants who didn't own their own land.

Perhaps this is one of the reasons that there is anti-philosophical tendency in Chan that comes from the way the early monks aligned their way of life to the way of life of illiterate Chinese peasants. After the farmer-monks finished working in the evening, they went back to the monastery and meditated in the Chan hall. A simple life. Working in the fields through the day. Meditating in the evening.

These monks also practiced meditation while they were farming. In Chan, your life is your practice. They meditated while they broke ground and sowed seeds. They meditated weeding and watering and tending their crops.

In Japanese Zen, this farming tradition of Chan becomes landscape cultivation, gardening, and the spare and beautiful Zen gardens. If we look carefully, we can see the rough agricultural roots of *nong chan* in the tremendous aesthetic refinement of the gardens in the monasteries of Kyoto.

It is no coincidence that in Buddhism we talk about the mind field, *xing tian*, an idea that is originally from the ancient Chinese Buddhist texts, not Sanskrit. We who teach Chan often use the mind field as a metaphor. We talk about softening the field's soil by removing rocks from it and, in the process, softening our hearts. Into this softened soil we sow the seeds of the Buddha's teaching.

We water the field with compassion. In Chinese we say, *Shui shi yi qie de yao mu*: "Water is the mother of all medicine."

The mind field is consciousness, the codependent arising of all phenomena. In order to grow this "field" and produce fruit from seeds, we need water, soil, and sunlight; many elements need to come together. The fruit cannot come out suddenly all by itself. Similarly, the mind field also needs to be cultivated and nurtured in order for the seeds of wisdom to sprout and grow.

Our minds are inseparable from the totality of all that exists. We share a common consciousness with *everything* else. Every leaf is Buddha. The river is Buddha's tongue and its sound is his voice.

If you want to help sentient beings, you have to get your hands dirty.

Just like farming.

Nong chan.

8

Floating

Swimming is like Chan. How do you learn how to swim? You first learn to float. And how do you float? You relax. You do nothing.

It can be frustrating when you're learning to swim. You flounder and flail. You sink and swallow water. When you're tense you're no longer buoyant. The more you try, the worse it gets. Chan is called the practice of no-practice. Don't do anything, and you will get it.

Babies are born with the ability to float. They float in the wombs of their mothers. We all want to go back to this original state. We want to relax and float.

If you look at how Chan masters teach, they are all different. But behind this multiplicity is a single purpose. They use every opportunity to bring their students back to their original nature.

No fixed way, no fixed form, the method of no-method. All of life is the teaching. Once you try to pin it down, make it this and not that, you sink. Relax. Be open, receptive, floating.

Chan Master Zhaozhou taught by telling people to go drink tea. Nanquan challenged his monks to say one true word about a cat. If they could not, he vowed to chop it in half. The monks were speechless, and Nanquan did as he had promised. But he only chopped the cat once; he didn't make a habit of it. Some Chan masters shout, scream, and punch.

These methods appear only once. The method of no-method. No fixed form. In another situation, the same Chan master would teach in a different way.

That is why we call Chan the methodless method.

The gateless gate.

This is the essence and spirit of Chan.

I MAKE THIS part of Chan sound very idealistic, very free. But that has not always been the case. As Chan evolved in China, it became formalized. Some people couldn't understand it or browse its meaning. As a result, we have great masters who codified the system and laid out the steps of the practice.

This was because, perhaps, some teachers were not so deep in their practice or students couldn't grasp the essence of the teachings. So you need form. You need appearances.

At Buddhism's beginning, when Buddha taught his disciples, they were guided only by these principles: Do all that is wholesome. Refrain from all that is unwholesome. Purify your mind. That is essence of the teaching.

People understood the spirit, the essence, in the beginning, but later on the spirit became elusive. As a result, the Buddha taught different ways of realizing this essence, and as a result, Buddhism has lots of precepts, rules regarding the regulation of behavior and thoughts.

Some people want to abandon the tradition. They want to reform and reconfigure without understanding the original spirit. That can be problematic. On the other hand, some people scrupulously follow tradition. They are rigid, don't adapt, and because of this, their practice loses relevance.

I think we need to follow tradition but make the tradition pertinent to the world today. We need to retain the spirit and lineage but change according to the needs of our time.

We should also have this attitude with our life when we engage with other people. We come back to the present moment with an open heart and open mind. We are buoyant. We go back to what we always knew. What we already had. We do nothing. No method. No form. We relax and float.

9

WISDOM

IN CHINESE, THE word for "wisdom" is *zhi hui*. It is composed of two characters: knowing and the sun. You can see; then you understand and know.

The Confucian idea of wisdom is complex. One of its primary applications has to do with wise governance. Confucius said if you want to govern the country, you start with the family; and to govern the family you have to first learn to govern yourself. Wisdom is about order and harmony, about ruling and pacifying.

The Chinese sense of wisdom colors Chan. Chan is intently focused on *prajna*, the Sanskrit word for "wisdom," which has been adopted generally by Buddhism. *Prajna*, as you might guess, also has multiple meanings. One of them is "to deliver," which is the way we use it when we vow to deliver sentient beings from suffering through skillful means. This is also called *bodhicitta*. *Prajna* can also be to see into the nature things—the essential emptiness that is at the root of Chan and the reality of co-origination, co-arising, flux, impermanence, and no-self.

In Chan, wisdom is coming back to the present moment. It is in the present moment that we see, smell, taste, feel, and think clearly. Our sense faculties open up and clarify. We see beyond the surface, beyond the superficial. We see birth, old age, sickness, and death as illusionary. We see nothing has a solid nature. We peel the onion, layer by layer. Everything is temporary. What is real? When you're in a good mood, everything is so pleasant. You delight in the songs of birds, the laughter of children. When you're in a bad mood, these same delightful sounds grate on your nerves. Which of these responses is real? Both are, of course. And both are not! Heaven and hell are states of mind. They have no intrinsic reality. Everything is relative. If we really apprehend this, we are on our way to wisdom.

A Chan disciple went to his teacher and wanted to attain purity of mind. The teacher asked him, "Who contaminated your mind and made it impure?" He heard his teacher's words and became enlightened.

On another occasion, a disciple went to the teacher and asked, "How do we attain freedom?"

"Who bound you up?" the master asked.

In Chan, we practice sitting meditation so we can maintain a level of focus and centeredness associated with *samadhi*. But you have to practice in order to maintain this stability of mind. If you stop meditating, it disappears.

This is not the case with wisdom. When you have wisdom, it is always there. Once you see something, you see it. And wisdom constantly deepens and clarifies.

Before Buddha became awakened, he was able to reach the highest or eighth level of *samadhi* where there is neither perception nor nonperception. And yet the Buddha was not liberated. When he came out of this state of *samadhi*, he still felt vexed. Buddha did not become awakened or liberated because of *samadhi* but because of wisdom.

So why do we practice meditation if Chan is about wisdom? Because without a certain foundation—*samadhi*—the mind will be scattered. If we light a candle in a room where the doors and windows are open and the wind blows through, the candle will flicker. It will not shine. The room will be dark.

Samadhi is the stillness of a sealed room—a state of peace and calm without disturbances that allows the light of wisdom to glow. It doesn't flicker. Slowly and steadily it becomes shining bright.

Wisdom is experiential. In Chan, we say it comes from returning again and again to the present moment. It comes from the experience of always returning. It comes from living this, from experiencing it for yourself.

Wisdom in Chan, and in Buddhism generally, is often divided into four stages. The first stage is wisdom from acquisition. This occurs through listening or reading. Then there is the wisdom of knowledge—to reflect on and digest what has been acquired. Practicing or putting into action the wisdom you have acquired is the wisdom of practice or cultivation. When you are able to fully experience what was been taught, this is called the wisdom of attainment.

There is a big difference between experiencing wisdom and becoming wisdom. At this last stage, there is no difference between you and wisdom. Wisdom is your life. Your actions, words, and thoughts are totally in accord with the Buddha's teaching. Wisdom is expressed in every action, by mere presence. This is the wisdom of full attainment. It is the Buddha inside all of us that is always there, waiting.

Like Buddha, when we have the wisdom of attainment, each word and every gesture will be a teaching.

10

HEN HATCHING EGG

IN THE CHAN practice of sitting meditation we cultivate a combination of patience, endurance, and tolerance. We can think of these qualities as a hen hatching an egg.

Have you seen a hen hatching an egg?

When she hatches the egg, what does she do?

She just sits. She sits and sits and sits.

How many days does it take for the egg to hatch?

Twenty-one.

When the hen hatches an egg does she mark the days—day one, day two, day three?

Does she look constantly at the time?

Does she ask how long it will take for the egg to crack open?

Does she wonder, "When will my chick be here?"

The hen doesn't look at day and night.

She just sits.

Does the hen become impatient?

Does she keep rubbing the egg so the chick will come out faster?

What does the hen do? She crawls very slowly and then gently sits. She settles herself comfortably into the nest.

Then she sits.

The hen has to be very mindful, very gentle, very slow.

When the hen is hungry, she goes and quickly eats some worms and then comes quickly back. If the hen is thirsty, she will not go drink water and start cackling with her neighbors. She will not eat worms and go walk around.

What does the hen do? She comes quickly back. She keeps hatching.

If you could speak hen language and ask the hen, "When will the chick come out?" the hen would reply, "I don't know. I just sit."

In Chan, we should be like the hen.

We just sit. And sit.

When we're sitting, we don't keep thinking: When will I become enlightened? When will I awaken? When will I not be sleepy? When will the pain stop? When will all these wandering and scattered thoughts disappear?

When the hen is hatching, look how relaxed she is! She is not tense or impatient. The hen does not say, "Enough! Enough sitting! Let's go for a rest and a night on the town. I need a break. Then I'll come back and finishing hatching."

Chan awakens us to patience, tolerance, and endurance. When you cultivate the virtue of patience, you become awake. You wake up your mind, you wake up your heart. You stop thinking, When will the egg crack? When will my chick come out?

You just sit.

11

THE VOW

I WAS A bit disheartened with Buddhism when I was in my late twenties. Not with the dharma or Chan practice, but with the petty politics of monastic orders and sects. I left Singapore to go to a university in Australia where I didn't know any Buddhists so that no one would come and bother me.

During this period in my life, my heart was shattered. I still intended to be a monk, but I thought I would study and perhaps become a lecturer or a professor at a university. Perhaps I would teach Buddhism, psychology, or sociology. When I left Singapore, I thought that I had left the land of my birth forever and would probably die in Australia.

During that time, I was not well-off. I went to the school to use the bathroom in order to save on toilet paper. Life was hard but meaningful, and I miss the simplicity of those days. There was an innocence about them. I was responsible only for myself. When you find meaning, even though you may be poor you are rich!

In retrospect, I think my plan of living on my own as a monk and becoming a university professor didn't work out because Avalokitesvara, the bodhisattva of compassion, didn't want to let go of me. I had made a vow to her, and that vow would eventually pull me back into an active religious life.

The vow came about in the following way. I was doing solitary practice in the mountains of Korea during the winter of 2000. Some Korean monks from a Chogye monastery south of Seoul led me on a four-hour hike to a small hut with no electricity or running water surrounded by snowy forest, far away from everyone and everything.

The hut was named Amrita, which means "elixir of life": if you drink it, you're supposed to be able to live forever. I had a woodstove for cooking and heat, and a bag of rice and big pot of kimchi on which I would subsist for one hundred days. I cooked my rice in water made from melting snow.

I was there to meditate. No reading, no writing, no walks in the forest—just meditation from before dawn into the night. The hut had thin shoji walls that rattled in the wind. It was very cold and snowed all the time. I meditated deep into the night with moonlight as my only companion.

Some weeks into the retreat, I realized I was getting sick. The sickness came out of nowhere and took me. The snow was very deep in the lonely mountains, and I had no idea where I was. It was impossible to find anyone for help. My fever rose, rolling over me in waves. I broke out in terrible itching suppurations. I had no medicine, and I was very weak. I realized I had the chicken pox, which could have been fatal for someone my age, in my late twenties. If you look at my right eyebrow now, you'll see a hole. It's said that pox leaves one mark. This hole is my reminder.

I knew that according to Chinese medicine, chicken pox can come from excessive heat, and I wondered if the heat inside me was being generated by all the blisteringly spicy kimchi I was eating. I was bundled up all the time against the cold, and the heat generated by the fiery kimchi had nowhere to go.

Perhaps the kimchi did contribute to my illness, but reflecting on it now, I see that I was also festering inside with the strong corrosive emotions of anger and resentment that came from my difficult experiences with the politics of Buddhism. I was sulking over my shattered heart. Perhaps the illness was a way my body and spirit were trying to purge those feelings.

The pox was truly awful. It was in my mouth, on my tongue, and in my ears. It covered my body from head to toe. It itched and burned. I felt like jumping out of my own skin. My fever soared. I had no medicine and grew weaker and weaker. I began to feel dizzy. The dizziness intensified, and then I collapsed. The wind swept over the Amrita hut, and the shoji shook. I lay shaking on the floor, wondering if I was going die.

I was angry at my body, angry at the illness, angry at the itching, angry at the lonely little hut and the isolation I felt. I was angry at Buddhist politics and all the petty ins and outs of the silly intrigues I had become embroiled in. And I was angry at myself for being angry! And then, lying there in my misery, I clearly saw that if I died an angry person, I would have wasted my life.

At the moment I prayed to Avalokitesvara. I told her that it would be a pity for me to die before I had accomplished my practice. I vowed to her that if I lived I was going to use my whole life for the propagation of Buddhism. Then I went into a coma.

I don't know how long I was unconscious, but when I woke up I felt a cooling sensation. Something had shifted inside me. I was at peace. I realized there was nothing to hold on to. The sad, angry, fearful feelings of my body dying, going away, left me. I felt that I could surrender myself and just let go of my body. I was ready to let go and embrace whatever was coming.

My teacher, Master Sheng Yen, has a wonderful story that illustrates how I felt. He was meditating on his solitary retreat in the hills of southern Taiwan when he saw a snake chasing a frog. The snake darted this way and that and the frog hopped ahead of it, just out of reach. Sheng Yen watched, fascinated, wondering if he should help the frog and restraining that impulse by reminding himself that the snake too had to eat. How would the chase end, he wondered? Would the frog manage to escape?

Then something happened that made a deep impression on him. The frog stopped and it turned to face the snake. The snake stopped as well. They just looked at each other for a long moment. Then the snake opened its mouth and the frog jumped in!

It was as though the frog was surrendering itself to the snake. It wasn't a suicide, only a realization that its time was up and the beauty of being able to die peacefully.

Coming out of my coma, I think I had the same feeling as the frog. I felt a great sense of relief. I felt very free.

12

Four Cups

It was said by the Buddha that to receive the teachings you should be like an empty cup. This is a well-known metaphor to Buddhists in the West. It is Shunryu Suzuki's teaching in his book *Zen Mind, Beginner's Mind*. The beginner's mind is the empty cup, open to possibilities, free from preconceptions. This was, for Suzuki, the Zen mind in the West. When he came from Japan to California in 1959, he saw the empty cup, the beginner's mind in Western students of Zen who were unencumbered by the long tradition of Zen and Chan in the East and the ways it had worked itself, often to the detriment of the vitality of practice, into the societies of China and Japan.

In Chan, although we also place importance on the empty cup and the beginner's mind, we use the metaphor of the cup in other ways as well.

In Chan, we should not only be empty, we should also avoid being like a cup that is contaminated with poison and dirt or a cup that is inverted or cracked.

Four cups.

LET US EXAMINE the first cup first.

What happens when a cup is full? Nothing new can be added. So if you are already full of your own ideas, you are not ready to learn. Empty your mind.

Chinese people have a saying: If three people go on a journey, one of them will be your teacher. There is always someone you can learn from.

Learning brings us joy. It is essential to our lives that we learn and grow, that we keep expanding ourselves.

You cannot approach Chan if your mind is like a full cup.

First cup, empty cup.

Cup number two is the soiled cup. If a cup is soiled with dirt or poison it will contaminate whatever good things you put into it. What are some types of dirt or poison? In Chan, we strive to keep our minds free from skepticism, suspicion, or assumptions. We strive to keep ourselves free from prejudices that stop us from seeing the goodness in others, which can lead to arrogance and pride.

The person who drinks from the soiled cup sees evil all around him. He feels persecuted, paranoid, and pessimistic.

Clean the cup of the mind.

Carefully wash and dry it well.

Third cup. This cup is inverted. Can you put anything inside it? No. If you invert the cup, nothing goes in.

That is the case when your motivation and purpose in life is impractical. When you are too naïve or idealistic. There is a Chinese saying for this: *Tou nao jian dan* (literally, "simple brained"). We have to be realistic about what we want in life and not be absorbed in illusions and fantasies. Get real! The inverted cup is an upside-down view—a view that is askew.

The fourth cup is cracked. You can still pour milk or water inside it, but whatever you put in will eventually leak out. We have to live wholeheartedly or what matters in our lives won't stay with us, whether it is learning or a relationship. In order to live wholeheartedly, we must find our own purpose, our own direction, apart from the expectations of our parents, husbands, wives, or friends. Our cup must be whole, not cracked.

If your cup is cracked, you will find that you're forgetful, unaware, and can't pay attention. Things will leak away and come and go. You have trouble with commitments. You will feel fractured, fragmented, and scattered.

How do we empty the cup, clean it, and make sure it's not inverted or cracked? By coming back to the present moment. By loving our breath. By practicing compassion. Slowly, slowly we clear our minds.

Empty the cup. And after you empty it, fill it with good things. Fill it with meal or honey. Then when we drink, we will truly be able to taste what we are drinking. Then we will get the taste of Chan.

13

GRASS ON THE FIRE

THE NATURE OF the student–teacher relationship in Chan distinguishes it from other religious traditions.

In Tibetan Buddhism, there is a type of practice known as guru yoga, which in Chinese is called *shang shi xieng ying fa*. It means to resonate with the teacher and follow his instructions totally. This will result in your mind and the mind of your teacher becoming one.

Tibetans ritualize the teacher–student relationship. The student visualizes the teacher and makes offerings to him. In Chan we don't ritualize the relationship in this way. Yet the relationship between the teacher and student is just as important. The student needs the teacher's guidance in order to have an awakening experience. The teacher does much more than impart knowledge. You can get Buddhist teachings on your own from reading and study. What the teacher transmits is the essence of Mind, which is not recorded in any book.

As is true in Tibetan Buddhism, in order to have

an intimate relationship with a teacher, you have to completely follow his instructions. Only then will you be able to see eye to eye, think mind to mind, feel heart to heart, and benefit.

Why is it that we have to so closely follow the teacher's commands? In Chan, we are not so much concerned with results; we focus on process. In the beginning of the relationship between teachers and students, some things may seem contradictory. It can be as though your teacher is a backseat driver. One moment the teacher tells you to go left, the next right. It can be maddening until you realize that on one side is a sheer drop and on the other a mountain of rock. You can't see these perils, but the teacher can. So we follow instructions; we follow the words.

In Chan, the teacher doesn't explain much. He says: Just do it! Don't worry about why. Go right. Go left. Just do it.

We must take care, however, about blindly following what a teacher says. Before you actually commit yourself to a teacher, you must trust him or her. You need to build and maintain a relationship.

The relationship between a teacher and a student is like any other relationship. It begins casually and becomes serious over time. When you commit in a relationship, what happens? You are responsible to the other party. It is the same with the teacher–student relationship, and the responsibility works both ways.

I tell my students to get to know me for five years. To see the good side and the ugly, the skinny and the fat. After they see everything, then they can decide to commit.

The opportunity to hear the teaching is precious, and the opportunity to encounter a teacher is also precious. Both are to be cherished.

I'M NOT SURE whether it is because of my karma, but I always seem to encounter my teachers during the last part of their lives, when they are already old and don't have much time left to teach me. As a result, I have always relied on my own to practice and taken advantage of every opportunity to question my teachers regarding my practice, and the instruction and wisdom they have been able to transmit has been particularly precious to me. I carry it with me always.

In this regard, I have always loved the following story. There was a dharma teacher, Xiangyan(?–898), who was revered for his expertise in the Diamond Sutra. He knew it inside out and used it in all his teachings. He had many disciples. One day his teacher, Guishan (771–853), a Chan master, came to him and asked him what has now become a famous koan.

"I'm going to ask you a question," he said. "You must answer me in your own words. Don't use any words that are found in the sutra. Before you were born, what was your original nature, your original face?"

The dharma teacher was in a state of shock. He didn't know how to answer the question. He went back to his room and looked through all the sutras, trying to crack the koan. Finally, he went back to the Chan master, kneeled down very respectfully, and bowed.

"I cannot find the answer," he said. "Will you please tell it to me?"

"That answer would be my answer," the teacher replied. "You must look for your own answer."

The dharma teacher went back to his room, packed his bags, and went off into the countryside, searching for the koan's answer. He traveled far and wide, and wherever he went he had the question in his mind that his teacher had given him: What is your original nature, your original face?

One day he arrived at a mountain where there was a deserted ruin of a monastery. The place was like his state of mind—like most people's minds. He started to tidy up. This cleaning and tidying up was a metaphor for his whole journey. The returning and returning and returning to the question.

He was sweeping energetically when he came upon a roof tile that had fallen on the stone floor.

With an energetic sweep, he sent the tile flying across the room. It cut across the space, hit the wall, and shattered.

The sound of the tile shattering awakened him.

He went outside the monastery, gathered dried grass, and made a fire. He put the bundle of grass on the fire, as though it were incense sticks, offering it in the direction of his teacher. And he made three prostrations in that direction as well.

He expressed his gratitude for his teacher for pushing him to find his own answer. In his wandering, he realized his teacher had always been with him, had, in fact, been teaching him the whole time. Because his teacher wouldn't give him the answer, he had to rely on his own effort and practice.

That parable is very close to my heart. Even though I am alone, my teachers are still teaching me.

14

COURAGE

WHERE DOES COURAGE come from? Very often we think that in order to be a courageous person, we need to use force, we have to fight and push. Actually, courage comes from being able to relax.

The Chinese root word for "courage" is *yong*. It means "strength," or "ordinary strength." Courage is not something extraordinary.

Courage is a sense of being grounded. That is where strength comes from. In Chinese, we say that Buddha had tremendous courage. We often call the main Chan Hall "the place of great courage and strength."

Most people think they have to find courage, that it is a thing to be found. But from the perspective of Buddhism, courage comes from doing away with fear. Most of us want to find courage to fight fear and overcome it. Courage then appears in the context of a struggle or fight. There is conflict, opposition—you want to oppose fear. That is how we usually think of courage, and as a result, we increase our problems.

Courage is a lack of fear in the face of danger, discomfort, hardship, or threats. The less scared you are of something, the more courage you have. Courage is a lack of fear. This is the practice of nonresistance. We do not resist. We do not retaliate. We do not react. We do not fight back.

This is a very Chinese idea that has its roots in Taoism as well as Buddhism. The Chinese Taoist martial art of *tai chi* is based on this principal. The *tai chi* martial artist doesn't counteract or resist when under attack. He goes with the flow. There is a Chinese saying: By using one ounce of energy, you can push one ton.

Tai chi movements are very relaxed, subtle, graceful, and flowing.

Tai chi is not only a martial art; it embodies an approach to living. It embraces a courage that is not about struggle and conflict but has a calm fluidity and powerful gentleness that is at the heart of the Chinese character and is the essence of Chan.

In the Heart Sutra we chant, "*Gate gate paragate parasamgate bodhi svaha.* Go, go, go beyond, go beyond the further shore." In Buddhism, we do not fight. We do not engage. This does not mean we're passive and condone injustice. When you become fearless you can truly make a difference when you see wrong being done.

In Chan, we transcend. In this way, there is no birth and no death. You go beyond, beyond the further shore. That is true courage. To not be afraid of death, the ending of life. That is courage. Stop fighting death and your own mortality. Accept impermanence. That is how to become fearless.

So simple, but is it easy?

Okay, it is easy.

Just relax.

15

GRACEFUL
EQUANIMITY

THE TEACHING OF impermanence is so strong in Buddhism, so fundamental. We all age and grow sick and die. You cannot stay young forever with Chan. Chan is not about the physical body, it is about the mind.

When he was in his late seventies, Master Sheng Yen was sick with kidney failure and was being treated with dialysis. His many disciples in Taiwan urged him to get a kidney transplant.

"You are a great master," they said. "It will benefit all of us for you to remain alive as long as possible."

Sheng Yen declined. He insisted whatever kidneys were available for transplant should go to a younger person, not someone who was already old and at the end of his life.

This is aging gracefully and facing death peacefully and with equanimity. Dying is natural. This is Chan.

WE CHINESE HAVE a saying that the Taoists don't eat the smoke and fire of the human world. They go into the mountains or into monasteries, purifying themselves and trying to attain immortality through esoteric practices. Chan taught a form of spiritual commitment as it took hold in China that provided another perspective, another way of looking at things.

Although Chan teaches that we are not our bodies, it also teaches that we still have to take care of the body and try to keep it healthy and strong. We talk of "regulating" and "harmonizing" the body. We use the word *tiao* in Chinese, which could be thought of as the process of finely tuning a radio receiver, turning it slightly this way and that until the signal comes in strong and clear.

Some practitioners have gone to the opposite extreme. They don't bother about the body; they don't take care of the body, and the body becomes sick. We need the body to realize ourselves and attain liberation. Chan does not believe in the repulsiveness of the body or that the body is an impediment. We work with the body and treat it as absolutely essential.

The first Buddhist vow is about this. We vow to deliver all sentient beings from suffering. "Deliver" has several meanings in this context. We think of ourselves as messengers "delivering" a parcel or message. We also think of ourselves as "delivering" people from one place to another. There is also the sense of being midwives "delivering" babies, or the Buddha that is in all of us. Like the midwife, we help the mother let go. Life is delivered through letting go.

Our physical bodies are precisely sentient beings. By loving and helping the self, we are able to love and help the rest of the creation, which in the Chan view is inseparable from our own self, our own body. If we are consumed by self-blame, self-hatred, or self-denial, then we can't hope to help others.

Although it is important to take care of the body, it is also important not to indulge it too much. We shouldn't fetishize the body. We need to be able to live with some pain in our lives. We need to be able to take some hits. Everything need not be so comfortable all the time. Wanting always to have absolute comfort is another extreme kind of attachment to the body.

In Chan and the teaching of the Buddhism we follow the middle path, the middle way. This comes directly from Buddha's experience.

MY STUDENTS ROUTINELY tell me that they hope I have a long life. Sometimes when I have been very sick, my students have been frightened that I would die, and they implored me to please live longer. My response is always the same: "The way for me to live longer is for you to practice Chan."

If no one wants to practice, what was the point of the Buddha staying in the world? "Who will be our teacher after you pass away?" his disciples asked him.

"The precepts," he replied. "Those who see the dharma see me."

Every moment is only one moment. Once that moment goes, will it ever come back? Every moment is the first moment and the last moment. That's why there's freshness in it. And because every moment is the last moment, we must cherish it. Its freshness is why it's wonderful. Its fleeting nature is why it's precious.

> *This day has passed, our lives too are closing.*
> *Like fish with little water.*
> *Pleasures will not last.*
> *Let us work with effort as if our heads are on fire.*

That is what we recite in the Chan hall during our evening service—these words of caution by Samantabhadra Bodhisattva. Our lives are evaporating away. Each breath brings us closer to death.

Once our life is gone, it is gone. It is just taken away. The sand runs through your fingers. You cannot hold on to this moment or any moment. There is nothing you can hold on to.

Life just goes, goes, goes. It doesn't stop. Still, our habitual mind thinks: there is still tomorrow, next week, next month, next year. Life is only as long as one breath. What if the next breath doesn't come?

When you face death, what is it that can help you? Chitchat? Gossip? A comfortable home? Power? Status? Money? Your family? No. Nothing and no one can help you. What can help is coming back to the present moment. The ability to always return to the present moment brings with it peace, clarity, and a brightness of the mind, even in the face of death. This clear, bright mind goes with you while you die.

16

TOK TOK CHENG

OVER THE YEARS in China, Buddhism deteriorated, and nowadays, among many Chinese, there is the impression that Buddhism is only about praying for the deceased.

Tok tok cheng is onomatopoeic Asian slang that mimics the sound of the striking of the wooden block and ringing of the bowls in Buddhist ritual. It makes fun of empty, silly services that became the way monasteries and monks supported themselves by officiating at funeral services, chanting, striking the block, and ringing the bowl. *Tok tok cheng.* This kind of empty commercialization of Buddhism and exploitation of the importance Chinese people put on funeral practices caused monks to become known as parasitic maggots and worms who live in and feed off the rice of others.

Funerals must be grand in China to signify that you are an important person. There can be thirty monks, all chanting, a full orchestra, lots of food, and offerings of all kinds. The belief is that chanting creates merit that accrues to the deceased and ensures a better rebirth. Professional mourners may be employed who beat their heads and weep, pound the floor and carry on, all for a fee. The monks are very much a part of this show, part of ushering the deceased through the ten halls of hell by burning joss paper and hell money (US one-dollar bills are popular these days; George Washington represents the king of hell who you are bribing to allow you to pass through the ten halls).

Chan became entwined with these cultural superstitions, and it was enmeshed in the way we Chinese believe that life and death are permeable and interconnected. The folk superstitions of China became the bread and butter of Chan monks and monasteries, much to the detriment of the religion.

But if you look at Chan, it doesn't talk so much about the dead. Its primary concern is what it is to be alive in the present moment. We say in Chan: "When you're alive take care of the living matters. When you die take care of the dying matters." Chan is about living a happier, more meaningful life. Not *tok tok cheng*.

17

MINDFULNESS
IN CHAN

FROM THE PERSPECTIVE of Chan, everything is spiritual practice, not only sitting on a meditation cushion. Practice is the moment you wake up until the moment you sleep, every single moment. How you brush your teeth, how you spit the water, how you pee, how you walk, how you close the door, how you eat—everything is a practice.

There is a Buddhist word for this in English: mindfulness. It has become very popular recently and has even moved outside the Buddhist sphere into realms that have more to do with Western psychology than Buddhism. The Buddhist practice of mindfulness originally comes from the Sutra of Mindfulness in the Pali Canon, which talks about mindfulness's four foundations. Buddha discussed these in his teaching, which became central in the Vipassana practices of the Theravada tradition.

Mindfulness has several meanings in Chan. One is simply to be attentive and aware. Which begs the question: What is it that we are attentive to and what should we aware of? In Chan practice, we have many types of mindfulness that apply not only to monasteries or on religious retreats but serve us well in daily life.

THE FIRST TYPE of mindfulness is mindfulness of time. What does that mean? It does not mean that you keep looking at your watch to see what time is it. Neither is it constantly looking at the clock and thinking, "When is my lunch break? I'm really hungry."

Mindfulness of time simply means to be aware of what is happening in the present moment. When we become aware of what is happening in the present moment, then we can actually engage with the present moment. And when we engage with the present moment, then we give attention to it.

In simple words, what does this mean? It's time for you to wake up, so you wake up. It's time to go to work, you go to work. When it's time to eat, eat; when it's time to sleep, sleep. In short, mindfulness of time simply means to be punctual.

Chan also practices mindfulness of space. You are attentive and give attention to space with your body, speech, and mind. For example, in your home you should be aware of the environment. Don't bump into walls. Don't stomp up and down the stairs. Return things to their place. Be mindful of space by replacing what you take from where you took it.

In Chan, we stress keeping your living area tidy and neat. When you wake up, you make your bed and tidy up the bedroom. When you use the living room or kitchen, don't leave things lying around. When you are leaving a place after you have used it, make sure it is clean and tidy. Leave it the way you found it. Turning off the light to save energy is mindfulness of space.

When you leave the room and close the door, do it slowly and gently so that you don't create a loud sound and disturb others. This is mindfulness of bodily action. Walk slowly and gently. This is also mindfulness of bodily action with regard to the relation of the space in which we live.

In our practice of mindfulness, there comes another quality of mind training, and we call this precision. In the cultivation of Chan, we have to be very precise. We pay attention to all the details. We are attentive.

Every step is a mindful step. Every moment is a mindful moment. Every breath is a mindful breath.

If you practice the mindfulness of breath, and yet your kitchen is a mess and your bed is unmade, that is a little bit weird.

Pay attention to detail; fold your towel; smooth the cover on your bed; scrub the kitchen counter;

clean the knives; put the cups away; hang up your clothes; don't drop things on the floor; sweep up your crumbs.

This is precisely what sustains our spiritual life.

I always tell my students and disciples that if you cannot even do small things, then you won't be able to accomplish much. Without attention to small details, big accomplishments aren't possible. Everything starts small and it goes a long way. That is why in Chinese we have a saying: "A fine stream of water will flow very far."

If there is a fine stream, lots of people can benefit from it: taking water, washing, bathing, cooking, and drinking. If there is a big gush of water in a flood, it destroys houses and devastates the land.

When we take care of every detail of our daily life that is the real spiritual practice. The practice becomes something real, not something that is separate from your life, separate from who you are. Very often people think that life is one thing and spiritual or religious practice is another. But that is not case in Chan. Our life is precisely the practice, and the practice is precisely this moment, the present moment.

Often our mind is very big, very ambitious. As a result, we don't take care of small things. We only want big things—the grand, the lofty, the transcendent. That is not Chan.

In Chan, everything is most important. Is there one moment that is more important than any other moment? No. Every moment is the same.

Take care of all details in your daily life mindfully with a gentle resolve.

18

OCEAN OF ENERGY

MOST OF US associate a relaxed state with comfort. You think when you're relaxed you're supposed to be comfortable. So when you feel discomfort, especially pain, that means you're not relaxed.

Thinking in this way can lead to all kinds of problems. Comfort is often a matter of habit and convenience, but it is not the way to become truly relaxed.

When I teach meditation, I spend a great deal of time talking about posture. Students new to meditation go through pain as they learn to sit. They want to amend the posture of a straight back and stable sitting base in the legs in order to be comfortable. I keep telling them: relax, relax, relax. But how are they supposed to relax when there is so much pain?

Muscles that are weak are also stiff. And muscles that are stiff are also weak. Why? In Chinese medicine we say the chi, or energy, is not flowing or maybe the circulation of blood isn't smooth.

Life has movement. Anything that becomes stiff and hard like a block of wood is dead. When there is this kind of hardness, the *chi* cannot circulate and you experience a certain numbness or soreness and, later on, pain.

The body is always trying to balance itself, to reach a state of balance. Just relax and the body will take care of itself. Relaxation can mean no force, no exertion; it also means no reaction—not to be angry, afraid, or upset when one feels pain.

Meditation students can experience a lot of numbness and soreness. The crossed legs they have been sitting on become so numb that they think they will never be able to use them again. Their legs become so numb they don't seem like their legs anymore. They can pinch them, hit them, and they don't feel a thing. I tell my students not to be frightened; in the history of Buddhism—for 2,500 years—no one has broken or fractured a leg because of sitting in meditation. For some people, that numbing can go through the body, into the torso or even the arms. The whole body can become numb. It can be a frightening feeling.

But in fact, this numbing is good: The body is trying to change itself. If you stay with it, the blood eventually goes through, and then there is no more pain. The *chi*, the energy, clears itself and you feel a certain sensation like ants crawling on your feet, back, legs, and hands. There are no ants! It is just the *chi* working.

In other cases, when people sit in meditation they may feel that suddenly their hands have become bloated or puffy. It's an illusion produced by the accumulation of *chi* in the palms. In Chan, after meditation, we do a full-body massage to spread any accumulations of *chi* that may have occurred throughout the body.

Some of these practices also come out of the Vedic yoga traditions, of course. They are not exclusively Chinese. But in Chan they have a distinctly Chinese style.

For example, when we meditate we place our palms on our legs and bring them close to the body, usually right below our navels. Our navel is called *chi hai*, or "ocean of energy." Placing our palm there helps to activate the ocean. In this way, Chan meditation utilizes principals from Chinese *chi kung*.

In meditation, people may find themselves crying, not out of pain and not because they're sad. They yawn and cry—these two things often go together. It doesn't matter. In Chan we understand it as the working of chi. Or some people may feel that they're expanding or shrinking, just like in the book *Alice in Wonderland*. Likewise, they may feel as though they're floating or sinking or tilting to the left or right. This is simply the movement of *chi*.

Chan is different in this way from other forms of Buddhism because it incorporates the Chinese understanding of the body and *chi* into its philosophy and practice. *Chi* has to do with energy and aliveness, and these are both essential to Chan.

19

Returning

Resting and relaxation are attitudes in Chan that we can carry from morning to night. I would like to introduce two more *R*'s—restlessness and returning.

In Chan, we practice returning. We return to the present moment. We return to our loyal friend, the breath. We return to our lives, which exist in the here and now. This practice of returning can be particularly helpful to you when you feel restless.

What is happening inside you when you feel restless? Your mind and body moves here, moves there. You wander off, you think about this, think about that. The mind is full of thoughts and it exhausts itself; you feel tired and fall asleep. After you finish sleeping, you wake up. You have energy. Then you start thinking again. So, for the whole day, there are three things you do: wandering thoughts, falling asleep, waking up, wandering thoughts, falling asleep again.

Or maybe you sleep the whole day; you don't know what's happened. The whole day you walk around tired; something is dragging you down. You feel dull and washed out. You can't focus. It is a big chore just to bend down to tie your shoe.

Restlessness is the opposite of rest. It can take many forms. It is not always hyperactivity or the inability to concentrate or settle down. Restlessness is also a state of depression, of sinking, of not being able to float. It is an exhausting tension, a state of conflict that can be more or less subtle.

You start thinking, "What's happening? Why am I like this? Why do I feel so tired and restless?" You are angry with yourself and disappointed. You feel you are wasting your life.

Perhaps you start blaming people. You grumble under your breath, "I feel this way because my husband snored all night. He wouldn't stop snoring. I was woken up so many times. *That* is why I'm so sleepy."

Or you blame the weather. It is too hot or too humid or too cold. There is high pressure or low pressure or it is going to snow. The snow has stopped, or there is too much wind. Or the wind is from the south or the west, or it is too still; the air is dead and listless and so are you. Or perhaps the planets are not aligned. It has to do with the planets and the season. In fall you get allergies, there's pollen in the air, and the planet Mercury is in such and such position.

When I lead meditation retreats, my students think they fail in their practice and start to find fault with everything. Their minds churn and churn. "What am I here for? Sit, sit, sit, sit. All I do is sit. Something must be wrong with my head. I paid money to come here and wash the toilet. Not only to wash the toilet, but to wake up at four o'clock each morning. And to sleep on a thin little mat on the hard floor. There is pain here, pain there, pain everywhere! Why I did pay to have so much pain? I must be crazy."

These thoughts are a form of restlessness. Their minds won't rest and settle. I tell them to relax. Come back to the present moment. As Thich Nhat Hanh says: "Breathe! You are alive."

IN CHAN WE talk about liveliness, not restlessness. There is no joy in restlessness, but the opposite is true of liveliness. The joy comes from the breath, from being alive, from touching life, from gratitude at the luckiness of living.

Chan is not detached or otherworldly. It's not about becoming immobile and inert. It's about coming back, returning to our true nature—our most instinctual, natural response to life. The essence of being alive is a feeling of vibrancy and immediacy. That is a very different state of mind than restlessness.

Come back to the present moment. Return to the breath. When we do that we don't feel restless. We feel relaxed. Calm and peaceful. Still. Settled. Stable. Alive!

20

PURPOSE

THE PURPOSE OF Chan practice is practice. It is not this goal or that goal. There is no goal in Chan!

There isn't something in Chan that we want to attain. Rather, through engaging with Chan or living Chan, you discover yourself, you become more aware of yourself. But at the end of the practice, you get nothing. There is nothing for you to get. Don't think: I want awakening. I want enlightenment. That is my goal. That is what I'm striving for. No! There is no goal. The Heart Sutra says, "No goal, no achievement, no attainment."

There is nothing to go after. There is nothing to get. We have to be very clear about our attitude and purpose.

Part of the process of Chan is to cultivate honesty. What is this honesty? It is the honesty of truth, to be truthful or true to yourself. Some people live in denial or fantasy or preconceived notions of the way the world is or how they want it to be. They do not want see parts of themselves that are ugly, dirty, selfish, or weak. But you have to see yourself for who you are. Only then can you accept yourself. That acceptance is the beginning of transformation.

When we say, "I want to be awakened, I want to be enlightened," what is it that we're awakened to? What is it that we are enlightened about? We discover the truth; we become awakened to reality.

We think, "I must be awakened to the truth. There is a reality I must discover. Then I'll become enlightened."

There isn't a special truth or reality that we awaken to. When you cultivate honesty, the truth is that we are sleepy! The reality is that we have wandering and scattered thoughts.

An honest mind helps us become aware.

Where is the truth? Where is the reality? The truth and the reality are in the present moment.

We learn to relax and accept the truth, the reality, whatever it is. Whatever is happening. Whatever situation and condition the body and mind are in. We are honest with ourselves. We accept things as they are. We relax. We do this over and over and over, from the moment we open our eyes until we sleep. We give ourselves to the process.

This is the purpose of Chan.

21

RESPECT FOR ANCESTORS

RESPECT FOR OUR ancestors is at the heart of both Chinese culture and Chan.

The reasons to offer respect and to keep our ancestors always in our minds are self-evident to us, but perhaps it seems a little strange to Westerners. What do we mean by respect for our ancestors, how does it apply to Chan, and what wisdom can we derive from it that is useful to us whether we are from China or the West?

In Chan we have what's called "paying tribute." On the new moon and full moon, twice a month, we pay respect to our lineage masters. We look into the essence of the virtue and the qualities that have been passed down to us. We acknowledge these qualities in ourselves, and we seek to pass them on to others.

This is very different than the traditional mode of Chinese ancestor worship, which is superficial and ritualistic and has a Confucian flavor of obedience and filial piety. In Chan, we venerate our lineage masters after a thorough investigation. We also pay respect to our lineage masters at the end of Chan retreats, when we can feel the qualities that have been passed down to us.

At the simplest level we seek to emulate the virtue of our ancestors in our minds, our hearts, our speech, and our actions. The word "virtue" in the West has a kind of self-righteous, holier-than-thou connotation. This is not the way we think of virtue in China. There are many ways to write "virtue" in Chinese. In the way I'm using it here, one side of the ideogram represents a double person; the other side is the character for "heart." Virtue can be thought of as having the heart of two people. You are able to feel and give more. You have extra compassion and empathy. It also implies courage.

When we seek to emulate the virtue of our ancestors it is not necessarily for their lofty ideals. If our grandmother was generous, the best way to pay respect to our grandmother is to be like her and be a generous person. If your grandfather was courageous, the best way to pay respect to your grandfather is to be a courageous person. Have that virtue in you.

In China, there are rituals that support this kind of respect, such as chanting or making an offering. There is nothing wrong with them; they are gestures, but they are not necessarily Chan if they are only for appearances.

The teachings of Chan are always about the heart and the mind. And Chan, as we have discussed, emphasizes daily life. You hold the qualities of those who have passed away in your heart and mind, and you also put those qualities into practice in the way that you live.

Respect for our ancestors in Chan also helps us have gratitude. It is part of our four great vows: to save sentient beings, cut off endless vexations, master limitless approaches to dharma, and attain supreme buddhahood.

If we're selfish, then we will not be able to give rise to vows. It is only when we are touched by others through gestures of love and kindness that we are able to turn ourselves in the direction of helping others. These gestures of love and kindness come most directly from our ancestors. In order for people to love others they must first experience love themselves.

In Chan, we also feel that it is our ancestors that have allowed us to come in contact with the Buddha's teaching. Without them we would not have the chance to overcome suffering and to help others do so. Because of that, we feel a profound gratitude. We bow deeply with respect. In Chinese we have a saying: "When you drink water, reflect on the source; when you eat fruit, bow to the tree."

When we recognize and acknowledge the source

of things we experience gratitude, and from this gratitude comes feelings of joy and peace. As a Chan monk, I am always aware of my teachers and all the other lineage masters and the Buddha from whom the teachings come. They all made sacrifices so I can learn Chan.

Our suffering was not caused by our parents or grandparents. It was merely passed down. We are social animals. We grow through modeling. We teach what we have learned. We act as we have been acted upon. A person who is not loving has not experienced love. It is not his fault. Realizing this gives rise to forgiveness. And in Chan we vow that suffering will stop with us. We will not pass it down.

Chan takes the folk religion of ancestor worship and the Confucian model of respect for our ancestors as fundamental to social continuity and harmony and adds to it and deepens it, helping us experience profound levels of gratitude, which gives rise to feelings of love and forgiveness. In its respect for ancestors, Chan emphasizes a spiritual lineage that goes back 2,500 years to the Buddha and celebrates the continuation of an ancient tradition of kindness and love.

22

Soft Kindness

Smile!

Integrate the smile into your life, smiling all the time, smiling each and every moment. By smiling, you relax your heart and mind. Smiling softens and opens you.

Smile to your breath. With each breath, smile. As you smile there is a certain calmness, serenity, tranquility, a certain friendliness, or *mitra*. This is *ci* in Chinese: a gentle, friendly, soft kindness, which can also mean generosity and giving or a positive regard.

As a result of *mitra*, the smile, you become closer to the breath; it is no longer something that is dead—it comes alive.

When you see a stranger and you want to make friends, what do you do? You smile to that person. By smiling, you start a relationship, and as you smile there is more warmth, more friendliness. As a result, the relationship will become closer and more intimate.

Mitra actually comes from another word in Sanskrit, *maitri*. In the Pali Canon, the standard collection of Buddhist scripture in the Theravada tradition, it is also known as *metta*. Most Buddhists in the West are probably more familiar with this term, which means "loving-kindness." In order for you to have *metta* or *maitri*, you have to make friends. If there is no friendliness, then it is difficult to have love and kindness.

The laughing Buddha—with his big, beautiful smile and big, jolly belly—is called Maitreya. His name derives from the word *maitri*, and he embodies the principal of warmth, friendship, loving-kindness. He is one big smile!

When we are sleepy, we smile; we are friendly to the sleepiness. When there are wandering and scattered thoughts, we smile. We smile to pain. We smile at our aches. We smile at our sickness. We smile when we fail. With all these things we make friends. We are friendly. When there is friendliness, all our suffering transforms. It is no longer the enemy.

Let's look at what happens when suffering becomes your enemy.

If suffering is your enemy, what happens? You have to fight; the whole day fighting. You try to push suffering away. You become very tense and agitated. It is exhausting! You constantly have to guard yourself against the enemy that may be coming to attack you.

If you smile and become friendly to your enemies, you establish a form of friendliness. When you no longer feel threatened, there is no threat. You feel secure and stable. And with this sense of security, you are better able to accept the present moment. You can come back to the breath.

On the other hand, when I say to be friendly, it doesn't mean that you play with wandering and scattered thoughts and the whole day you are busy making friends. Or you become pals with sleepiness and you fall asleep, and you and your new friend sleepiness have a nice, long nap together. To have a sense of friendliness simply means there is no enmity, no threat, no bad feelings. So you are friends, and as a result, when your friends are around you feel comfortable. You feel very comfortable and relaxed. And you stay in the present moment.

23

LET IT COME,
LET IT GO

WE DO NOT try to chase after, run after, grasp anything. Nor do we try to resist or push away or reject anything. So this is how the mind relaxes itself from wandering and scattered thoughts.

When you grasp or resist, you end up trying to materialize your spiritual practice. Trungpa Rinpoche brought this idea to the West when he wrote *Cutting Through Spiritual Materialism*.

The materialistic mind can be dangerous because we end up calculating. We become calculating, and then we discriminate. The mind will discriminate, judge, and end up biased.

Grasping and rejection work in the following way: We have ideas of good and bad, which result in likes and dislikes. This results in what we call a dualistic mind or the mind of opposition. Owing to opposition, there is conflict and contradiction. There is no harmony or balance. And when there is no harmony, there is also no peace.

When our minds aren't peaceful we will constantly engage in extreme views. On one hand, we are chasing after the good. On the other, we are resisting, pushing away what seems to be bad. So the mind is constantly moving, moving, moving, moving. The whole day is like a bullfight.

When the mind will not settle, we keep wanting to chase after a state of peace, where there are no more wandering and scattered thoughts, no more restlessness or lethargy, no more anger or distress, no more suffering or vexations. We want this, we want that. So there is greed. There is craving. We attach, we try to grasp, we try to hold on, and we become tense.

Or we try to push away, we try to resist, we try to fight wandering and scattered thoughts. When they come, we fight them. We try to push them away as you would try to push away your sleepiness. You get frustrated and angry and become even more tired and tense.

All this tension and pressure builds up and results in an imbalance, a lack of harmony. You are no longer peaceful. You can't settle down. This is the cause of *duhkha*, the Sanskrit word that means "vexations" or "suffering." It is the cause of all unhappiness. We can never get what we're chasing. It doesn't matter if we want to create or not create. We want a certain type of state of mind—happiness, joy, and serenity. Or we want a mind free from restlessness and pain. In both cases, we are grasping or rejecting and chasing after the impossible.

Just relax and smile. The more we try to get the result we think we want, the more we agitate whatever is bothering us and actually impeding us. It is like a fishpond: the more you stir it up, the murkier it gets. We should not be so reactive. But that doesn't mean to be nonreactive. It means we should seek to be *pro*active. Even before problems arise we become aware of them and let them go. By reacting we only create new problems. Whenever you grasp at or push away or reject, you live in the world of opposites and duality. You have conflict and tension.

If you take this tendency to its endpoint you have, on one hand, the craving for existence, which is *bhava*, and on the other hand, the craving for nonexistence, which we call *vibhava*. We are trying to create the existence of what we crave and the nonexistence of what we resist.

Relax. Come back to the breath. Come back to the present moment. Don't try to chase after, hold on to, grasp. Don't try to resist, push away, or reject. Just relax. Breathe. Whatever comes, let it come. And then let it go.

24

THE WATERFALL

SOMETIMES I CRY when I meditate. I cry because there is a feeling of connection. When I go deep into my practice, I touch the ground, the great earth, all that is.

I connect to all those who are breathing, all those who are gasping for breath, all those who are drowning or breathing their last breaths on their deathbeds, all those who are panting in sickness or trying hard to breathe because they are old and every movement hurts. I connect with the newborn's first breath of life, that beautiful first breath that exchanges itself with the world. I connect with the mother, whispering and cooing to her baby, holding it so close. They are exchanging breath, their breath is mingled in the way the breath must mingle in the kiss of young lovers, and although as a monk I have never had that kiss, I connect with the lovers too.

The plants are breathing, exchanging waste and transforming it into the air we breathe. They are breathing in and out, quietly and gently infusing the air, making it delicious, making it good. We are cradled in the great lap of the world, which holds us close, as close as the mother holds her child, as close as the lovers hold each other.

Intimacy and love are all around us. The beauty of life is beyond words. It is so profound and yet so simple. I touch it and at the same time it is deeply touching me. This present moment is a common moment. How many lives come and how much life goes? Right here, right now; appearing and disappearing; coming and going; arising and falling away. The tears come from my overflowing heart.

It is as Thich Nhat Hanh says: "I have arrived; I am home."

I like to say: "Home at last!"

This is my refuge.

I also have tears when there are feelings of gratitude toward my teachers or the triple gem—the Buddha, dharma, and Sangha. The Sangha is not just the group of people you practice Buddhism with or our human community: it is all beings—the rivers, trees, mountains, forests.

Everything is teaching us. Constantly.

This realization brings with it an overwhelming feeling of gratitude. It is as though I have been blind for millions of years. The whole world has been dark and suddenly someone has brought a lamp.

All the lineage masters appear and I can clearly see them in a long line, a totem going backward in time, a tree with countless graceful branches, a waterfall of ceaselessly flowing love and compassion from those who have come before me, who have taken the posture, who touched the great earth. It is a reunion, a congregation of the compassion that has accumulated for 2,500 years. It is full of the gentlest, kindest, most tender energy. It is so pure in its good intention, so cleansing, so cooling, like swimming in a cool stream on a blazing hot day.

The tears come from the gratitude for the greatest gift—the gift of life, our plain and simple ordinary life: the sun, the moon, the stars, the great earth, the breath—all so ordinary, so available, nothing mysterious. And yet, each moment, a miracle.

25

SKY MIND

The sky can accommodate anything
Birds cut through the sky
Or a plane
The sky comes back
It is as it is
Effortless, whole
Volcanoes erupt
Forests burn
The sky is not burned
Nothing added
Taken away
Boundless and vast
Tornados, hurricanes, typhoons
Planets collide
The sky accommodates
Sun and moon
The countless stars
Bodhisattva of the great earth!
Bodhisattva of sky!
Widen our reach
To embrace and put our arms around

26

SALT AND SHEEP

To BE AWARE is to be constantly in the present moment, fully relaxed. In Chan meditation, you try and try and try. You know you fail; you try again. You know you are trying, and then you relax and come back into the present moment.

You can get a taste of this kind of awareness by sitting comfortably wherever you are and becoming aware of your body, of your heartbeat, and the movement of your chest and abdomen as you breathe. Let your breath fall into its natural rhythm. Relax into its rising and falling.

With practice, you will find that you can actually touch your breath. Not put your hand on it but become aware of it. And with awareness of the breath comes a deeper relaxation. You feel the natural rhythm of the breath.

Some people learning meditation hear the word "concentration," and they take it to mean to concentrate or to focus. As a result, they force themselves to *concentrate*! This creates pressure.

The body and mind are tight. Energy is being expended, gobbled up, and this creates a kind of nervous exhaustion.

In Chan, concentration refers to a quality of mind. It is not attained by force or an assertion of will. Rather, it refers to our *density* of mind.

What do I mean by "density"? Think of it as being more or less diluted. For example, think of a handful of salt dissolved in water. How can we obtain the salt? One way is to put a small fire under the water and slowly boil it off. As the water evaporates, the salt solution becomes more and more concentrated. This too happens with density of mind. Concentration, in this case, is not a verb. It is not an action. It refers to a quality. It is the salt.

This is how the mind progresses: It's initially scattered, mixed up, all over the place. We filter; we refine; we concentrate. Our awareness also thickens like this. It becomes concentrated. The wandering and scattered thoughts are the water evaporating. We just let them go.

IN CHAN, WE work with the mind from two aspects: the *scope* of the mind and the *activity* of the mind.

We round up the mind like a sheepdog herding sheep.

In the morning, the sheep are all over the place, eating grass here and there. The shepherd lets out the sheepdog, a clever, skillful creature. The dog dashes around, making circles that are smaller and smaller to gather the sheep.

The mind is like the sheep—all over the place, scattered over a large area. Coming back into the present moment brings our minds back to a smaller area, which is the body. This is what I mean when I talk about the scope of the mind.

Likewise, activity of mind is a gathering process. Chan sees the untrained mind as haphazardly moving. By coming back to the present moment, by coming back to our bodies and breath, we train the mind to move in a regular pattern in a small area until we are able to slow it down and eventually bring it to a single point. Our awareness is in that single point: it is very concentrated, very dense. When this happens, a natural rhythm emerges that is no longer self-imposed. It is not self-created. It exists *prior to the self.*

When you are bringing your awareness back to the present moment, back to the body and breath, you are still working. You are still self-generating and self-creating. There is effort involved and pressure. This kind of relaxation is not very relaxed. There is intention. You are looking for the breath instead of finding the breath and letting it come to you.

You will discover that if you keep coming back to the present moment, if you keep coming back to the breath, you will train the sheep. As soon as they see the dog, they come together all on their own and gather themselves into an obedient little group.

We have evaporated the water. The salt is in hand. The sheep are nicely arranged. In this state, awareness is what we are. Still, in Chan we go one step further. After we concentrate and become awareness, we ask: Where does this awareness come from? What's behind the veil?

27

THE WAY OUT

WE OFTEN TALK in Chan about wandering and scattered thoughts that keep the mind from slowing down and resting. These thoughts, however, are only part of what distracts us in any given moment. Mental pictures or images may also distract us by capturing our attention. Or we may be distracted by sounds, melodies, or smells—anything, in fact, which stimulates the senses. If no words attach to these sensory phenomena, they're simply music, taste, smell, or image. If words attach, we call them thoughts.

A thought comes when you hear something—a dog barking, for example. You start talking to yourself and create a storyline. What color is the dog? How big is it? How old is it? Is it male or female? You remember the dog you had as child, how the two of you played together, the fondness the dog had for cheese doodles. And so forth. This goes on and on until the mind tires of playing with it and moves on to other things. In the meantime, there is a storyline. These are thoughts, and this is what in Chan we call "thinking."

Thoughts may trigger feelings. You hear the dog barking and then instead of wondering about the dog's color, you become irritated. The dog's barking sets you on edge. You become angry, and the story in your mind now involves taking a stick to the dog.

Emotions don't always start with thoughts. It's chicken and egg. Thoughts arise from emotions. You hear the dog barking and grow sad. The barking dog reminds you that your dog recently died. The dog was a wonderful friend, and you think of all the fun you had together. Thoughts arise and keep arising, and the more you think the sadder you become. The emotion of sadness kindled by the dog barking is followed by thoughts, and these thoughts enforce the emotion, which magnifies. You have more thoughts, and in the end you start crying. You sit there and cry.

Emotions generate thoughts and thoughts generate emotion. It's like a cycle, a vicious cycle. What is the way out? Relax. Train the mind. Come back to the breath. Breathe! And come back to the present moment.

28

CHANGING OUR MINDS

WE HAVE THOUGHT very carefully in Chan about being able to feel your breath, relaxing into your breath, and becoming absorbed and dissolving into the sensation of the breath.

In the Anapanasati Sutra, the Buddha talks about mindfulness of the body and breath, and this was elaborated on over the centuries in Chan. Chan incorporated into itself some sophisticated and often esoteric Taoist explorations (which predate Chinese Buddhism) of chi, the energy of the cosmos that circulates through our bodies. Chan's roots are also in the Vedic teachings of India, which also predate Buddhism and in which the Buddha was well versed.

To breathe is a miracle—the first condition of life. The breath is our primary bridge, the way we interact with the external world. It is the way we connect with others. We all breathe the same air, just as we all walk the same earth and drink the same water.

As we experience the subtle nature of our breath, and we use our breath to bring us over and over again into the present moment, we see that we feel time because of a chain of thoughts, the current of thought. A thought comes and then goes away. Then the next thought comes and goes away. As a result, there is the past thought, the present thought, and the future thought. One thought after another. This is what creates the sense of time passing.

If we are in the present moment, only the present moment, then there are not a lot of wandering and scattered thoughts. We are always in the here and now. As a result, we don't feel time. That is why an hour can feel like less than a minute.

In this state, we forget about time. We forget about space. We forget about what's going on around us. There is only the breath. We don't seem to hear or smell—only the breath, in and out, in and out. We forget our body. This can become frightening for people. Suddenly we don't feel our arms or legs, or the whole body disappears. It's as though the body dissolves into air, becomes hollow, like a shell. We have what we call a state of ease. In Chinese the term is *qin an*. Body and mind become totally at ease.

We can devote ourselves to the potential of our breath in our daily lives. By bringing ourselves back to the flow of our breath we can begin to feel that natural, effortless flow in our jobs and relationships. If we stick to the breath, at the end of the day we will feel lighthearted, *qin an*—a feeling of serenity, peace, and calm. This is Chan—not sitting on a cushion meditating and experiencing the breath, but bringing the breath wholeheartedly in our daily lives, into the world.

In Chinese, *qin* literally means the sensation of weightlessness. *An* is a feeling of stability. Weightless stability. How is this possible? Usually, for us to feel stable, we need to feel weight. When we experience *qin an*, however, we are stable but we don't feel weight. We are light, weightless, but we feel very steady, very stable. If this is hard to imagine, think of an elephant. When you see an elephant walking it is very steady, not at all clumsy. You can feel its stability. And so it is in this state: you feel very steady, you feel whole, of one whole piece.

It is a new and strange and wonderful feeling when it happens, because our minds are usually so scattered and discombobulated. In Chan we are careful to distinguish this state from *sunyata*, or emptiness. It is a state of concentration or absorption. It is still the elephant. It is still the self, although the self is unified with the external. In Chan, we shatter this state of unified mind to arrive at no-mind, *sunyata*—enlightenment.

When we experience *qin an* we are free from all our aches and pains. This is part of the feeling of lightness. Pain brings with it a feeling of heaviness, of being trapped, confined, and out of control; the centrifugal force of pain bears down on us, crushing us back into our bodies, causing our muscles to be heavy and tense.

In the state of absorption, we don't feel pain. We are comfortable and relaxed. We can sit for hours in meditation and feel no pain or numbness; we are airy, light, serene, and calm. Does that mean our aches and pains disappear? Unfortunately, no. When we come out of the absorbed state, pain will come back because our bodies are made of flesh.

Also, when we're in this state, we don't seem to have any wandering and scattered thoughts. Does that mean the wandering and scattered thoughts disappear? No. It simply means that because you are absorbed, you no longer pay attention to them. They only seem to disappear.

Unless you are a corpse, there will always be mental activity. It's a matter of more or less. The sensation of less and less wandering and scattered thoughts comes as you train yourself to focus more of your attention on the present moment.

If your mind is captured by what you're reading, you may enter what we call in Chan a state of preabsorption. You may have ceased to be aware of your surroundings, which for me, as I write this in the lush hills south of Jakarta, is the sound of rustling leaves, the wind blowing, birds singing, and water tumbling over stones in the stream below.

In the state of preabsorption, you begin to lose the sense of time, space, and your body. You lose the sense of thoughts and surroundings. Before all this happens, you actually become aware that your breath changes.

How does it change?

Generally, breathing is a cycle of sixteen breaths per minute. As we enter the absorbed state, each breath lengthens and can seem to go on forever, which can be disconcerting. The exhale goes on and on. Is it ever going to end? In the absorbed state we typically have four rather than sixteen breaths per minute.

No matter what you're doing, come back to the breath, come back to the present moment. Through the experience of the breath we will always find hope. The breath transforms heaviness into lightness, chaos into order. With our breath, we can change our minds. When we can feel our breath we become alive whether we're walking, sitting, eating, or doing the dishes. We can experience absorption and find a state of serenity and peace.

Happiness does not come through external stimulation and excitement. Happiness is found within. It arises naturally from becoming absorbed, from *qin an*. Happiness arises from peace, and peace comes from practicing bringing your mind to the present moment, from coming back to your breath. It is an art. It is about doing and creating. And it starts with the breath.

29

WOMB BREATHING

IN CHAN MEDITATION, when you refine the breath to a certain point you may develop what's called "womb breathing." The Taoists have practices to deliberately attain this state, but in Chan meditation it happens by accident.

When you breath in this way, it is as if you are a baby in the womb. The baby doesn't use its nose, mouth, or lungs to breathe. It breathes through the umbilical cord in its navel that connects it to its mother.

In womb breathing, we don't use an umbilical cord, but our chest is no longer breathing. It is as if every pore of our body breathes. When we exhale, the air goes out of all our pores. When we inhale, our pores absorb the air like a sponge.

Although this happens accidentally in Chan, it shows how rooted Chan is in the subtleties of our breath and physical bodies. Chan is like climbing a tree. You are trying to get to the top; along the way there are branches that you could go up, but these are diversions from your goal. In Chan, if we experience womb breathing we don't make a big deal out of it. We don't progress in that direction through our awareness or intention. We don't try to deepen or magnify the experience. Our goal is rather to go back to what we were doing, coming back to the present moment and refining our minds. We don't pay much attention to breathing through our pores.

30

Turtle Breathing

A LAST TYPE of breathing that may occur in Chan meditation is called "turtle breathing." In Taoism, as with womb breathing, this practice is done deliberately. In Chan meditation, it can happen by accident.

There is a certain type of turtle that buries itself in the ground for long periods. How does the turtle survive? It becomes its own little cosmos, a self-contained, self-sufficient unit with no need for oxygen or other external nutrients to keep it alive.

The same thing can happen when highly accomplished Chan masters go into deep *samadhi*, a very deep state of absorption. You can't feel their heartbeat or breath. It seems as though they are dead, but they are actually able to sustain themselves. We call this the turtle breathing, a practice similar to Indian yogis who can stay underwater for long periods of time.

Sheng Yen's grand master and my great-grand master, Empty Cloud, was giving a public talk in

Thailand on the Universal Gates in the Lotus Sutra. During the talk, he went into deep *samadhi*, sitting motionless and perfectly still. A day and night passed and still he sat. News of this remarkable feat spread. Even the king came to pay respects. Empty Cloud finally came out of *samadhi* after nine days.

Although Empty Cloud was a Chan master, in Chan we don't encourage this type of training. This ability might seem marvelous and supernatural, but from a Buddhist perspective it's no big deal. It can also lead to trouble.

I think particularly of the rather hair-raising near cremation of Chan Master Guang Qin in Taiwan. Lychee farmers working in the fields saw him sitting in a cave. After several days when he hadn't moved they thought they should investigate. He was perfectly still, without a heartbeat, and didn't seem to be breathing. They assumed he had died and built a fire, intending to cremate him!

Fortunately, news of this reached Master Hong Yi, who hurried to the cave and rang a bell, bringing Guang Qin out of his deep state of absorption. I think the moral of this story is to be careful of turtle breathing. You could find yourself coming out of meditation on your own funeral pyre!

31

PROSTRATIONS

USUALLY, I DON'T have any big problems. But occasionally something comes up. Thinking doesn't help because the problem is too big. It is beyond me. It has to do with my monastery or congregation, or the religion generally and how it fits into the larger society of Singapore or some of the other places I go to teach. So I do prostrations to Kuan Yin or Avalokitesvara, the bodhisattva of compassion. Her name means "deep listening" or "contemplating the universal sound." I am mindful of my body. I move very slowly, like the characters in the movie *The Matrix* when they are dodging bullets.

Dung, dung, dung, dung.

This is the Chan Matrix. Very slow. Very mindful.

After a while, I calm down.

THERE ARE SOME things that are simply beyond us, beyond our ability to control or understand. Buddhism is sometimes called "a science of mind" rather than a pure religion, although it has religious aspects. Religions always believe in a creator God. Not Buddhism. Buddha was a man, not a god. He did not create the world. In Buddhism there is no one pure being above everything else.

I was brought up as a scientist. I studied biotechnology and majored in genetic engineering. I was attracted to science because I wanted to understand why things are the way they are. I wanted to probe their deeper meaning. That's what attracted me to genetics. Why are we all different? Why do twins with the same parents and upbringing differ in personality and behavior? Why are some people born black, white, or yellow? What are these tiny strips of carbon, DNA and RNA, which make this self seem so real? How can a tiny sperm and egg come together and make a full-grown human being who can think and feel? Where does the self come from? Where does it go? These were the questions that propelled me into science.

I soon came to see that science, with all its deep understanding of how the material universe functions, could not answer fundamental questions of why things are the way they are. I became curious about religion and read in the various traditions of religion and philosophy. I joined Buddhist, Muslim, Catholic, and Hindu societies in Singapore, looking for answers. When

I was exposed to Buddhism, it was like striking a big bell. There was an immediate resonance.

I loved that Buddhism, like science, was empirical. You experienced it for yourself. You tested its tenets by turning the mind inward, by self-examination. I was impressed by the ways in which it jibed with science. Buddha talked about relativity 2,500 years ago, the ceaseless flux between matter and energy, the changeableness of everything in the universe, the idea that matter is actually emptiness, and things that are seemingly solid are really insubstantial.

I was also touched by the Buddha's story. He had been born a prince in the lap of luxury. This was very impressive to a teenager from a simple Chinese Singapore family. He had given up his kingdom and all the comforts of life to search for truth and to help people. He had led a simple and selfless life.

"What am I going to do with my life?" I asked myself. I saw my future mapped out: family, work, mortgage, bringing up kids, retire, get old, get sick, die. "What is the point of it all?" I wondered. When I heard about the Buddha's life, I thought that perhaps I could make a difference by following in his footsteps. I was attracted by his wisdom and moved by his compassion. I too wanted to lead a noble and selfless life of service. The Chan spirit grabbed me.

My motives sound very pure and high-minded,

but I have to confess that part of what attracted me to Buddhism and becoming a monk were the Shaolin kung fu movies to which I was addicted as a boy. The monks enchanted me with their fighting prowess and their otherworldly spiritual power. I would walk around the house with a blanket draped over my shoulders as if it were a monastic robe. I played at kung fu, kicking and punching, jumping up and down on my bed and grunting and shouting with fierce martial sounds. I was always asking my mother to shave my head. I wanted the look and garb and a child's cartoonish idea of holiness and power.

Let's say Chan was a calling and leave it at that.

I FIRST DID prostrations in my teenage years and started regular prostration practice when I was sixteen or seventeen. Prostrations have been an essential part of my practice ever since.

There are benefits of prostrations that have nothing to do with a working out of karma or tapping into the beneficence of a supernatural power. Prostrations help our circulation. When you prostrate, blood flows to the head. After prostrations, your thinking sharpens. Going down to the floor stretches your spine, and the flow of *chi* improves. The slow movements of prostrations are mindful, and so you relax and your mind clears up.

Westerners are suspicious of prostrations, which

smacks to them of idol worship, which is distasteful at best. After all, you are bowing down before a statue. Not only bowing, but actually supplicating yourself fully on the floor. There's a groveling Oriental obeisance to the posture that offends the egalitarian and individualistic Western sensibility.

But from the Chan perspective, prostration is an art, a highly developed spiritual technology that is beautiful and profound.

The statue is a symbol, an object of our awareness. We stand before it and bring our fingers together at our chest, at our heart. We center ourselves. Our ten fingers represent the ten realms of existence—six unawakened and four awakened.

The unawakened realms are hell; hungry ghosts; animals; demigods (*asuras*); *devas*, or gods; and the human realm. The awakened realms are the *arhats*, enlightened beings; the *pratyekabuddhas*; bodhisattvas; and the buddhas.

These ten types of beings comprise existence. Bringing our fingers together over our hearts signifies that our state of mind and our hearts create our reality, our heaven and hell.

We all experience the greed of hungry ghosts; the ignorance of animals; and the jealousy and conflict of *asuras*, whose males are ugly, coarse, and always doing battle with each other, and whose females are beautiful, seductive and cause no end of trouble. We are also the *devas*, who indulge in life's pleasures, sensual beings who are always merrymaking. Our human selves are a mixture of all this.

In the awakened realm we have the *arhats*, the renunciants, who have attained the goal of religious life by letting go: through nonattachment, through the wisdom of impermanence and no-self. The *pratyekabuddhas*, beings who have attained enlightenment by themselves, often appear in nature. Their wisdom comes from *sunyata*, emptiness, codependence and co-arising, whereas the *arhats* attain wisdom through impermanence and no-self. Bodhisattvas are awakened beings with all these qualities, but they also have great compassion and love, and they help sentient beings. The buddhas are a completion of wisdom.

We are mindful of these realms and their subtleties as we begin our prostrations and our ten fingers touch, creating hell or heaven in the here and now.

In the center of our palm is a space, which represents emptiness. Everything is created in the here and now, and emptiness is the true nature of our hearts and minds. As we stand to begin our prostration we have the awareness that what is here and now is only our state of mind, and whatever it is can change. We can change it.

We bow and make a *mudra* by the wrapping the palm of our left hand over the fist of the right; our two index fingers come up to touch each other. The shape of our hands represents the lotus bud, the lotus bloom in Buddhism that symbolizes the beautiful, fragrant flower of wisdom and compassion—buddhahood—that grows out of the mud of *samsara*, the endless cycle of death, rebirth, and suffering to which the material world is bound.

We bow to signify humility, the humble, transforming the mind. We are like buds; we too can be transformed; we are buddhas-to-be.

We bring our hands up to level of the eyes. Our eyes see the bud. It represents offering, generosity, respect. The bud is our heart and we offer it to all sentient beings who are all manifestations of Buddha. We learn to truly see others, to communicate and reconcile. How many of our problems come because we cannot see eye to eye? The lotus bud before our eyes reminds us of this.

Then we clasp our palms again and prostrate to the ground. Our hands and arms are out in front of us. We touch the earth like a lightning rod. We ground ourselves.

This part of the prostration is what may be particularly unseemly to some Westerners. Our supine posture represents renunciation. We let go of the ego, of our arrogance and pride, the cause of so many of our problems. This is the beginning of wisdom.

We turn our open palms, which are our open hearts and minds, upward to receive wisdom and compassion. We close our palms to bring in the wisdom and compassion to our hearts and minds. We turn the palms around to touch the earth with all its dirt and muck, all those things we suppress, that we don't want to face, that we sweep under the carpet. In Buddhism, we transform by facing the dirt, by touching it. We touch it with wisdom and compassion.

As we slowly stand, we are the lotus coming up out of the muck, out of the dirt, starting again, fresh and new. We have transformed our hearts and minds. We have transformed troubled relationships and this troubled world.

In our prostrations, by purifying our mind, we purify the world. We build the Pure Land. We touch the sick, the suffering, those who are lost in grief, frustration, and despair. We touch the dying. We touch everyone with wisdom and compassion. We connect all of life with humility, generosity, and respect. We touch the great earth.

THE PROSTRATION PRACTICE I have described comes from different sources. You can see the Indian and Vedic influence, which were consonant with Chinese folk beliefs. Chinese folk beliefs also contain the theology of the six unawakened realms and the idea of heaven and hell. The awakened realms are uniquely Buddhist and come into China and down through Chan practice intact through the centuries.

Kuan Yin enters Chinese folk religion as a kind of intermediary, a messenger, who might be thought of as akin to Athena, between the Buddha and the Jade Emperor, who is the Zeus-like ruler of the Chinese pantheon in heaven. Kuan Yin comes out of the bamboo grove where she resides to pacify and calm the Jade Emperor and sooth the relations between heaven and earth. In folk religion, the Buddha abides in the Western Land, a remote, transcendent figure who only intercedes in human affairs during times of extreme crisis. The rest of the time he leaves trouble, heartache, and strife to the goddess of compassion in her bamboo grove.

I was born on Kuan Yin's birthday, and my mother brought a statue of her into the house. Like many simple Chinese women, she prayed to Kuan Yin when she had troubles, humbly imploring the goddess to help her. My prostration practice to Kuan Yin could be thought of as just another form of this kind of simple act of devotion.

The height of my prostration process came in Korea where I participated in a special Son retreat practice—300,000 prostrations in 100 days. It takes about twenty minutes to do a cycle of 108 prostrations; to do the 3,000 a day required by the retreat required about nine hours. It was a spring and fall retreat, and you could break it up (although the Koreans like to do it in one block), moving from monastery to monastery for stretches of one week to a month. The monasteries will give you a little room in which to prostrate or a space in the hall.

I did part of the retreat in the spring, then did a *Kyol Che* retreat in the summer, and finished the prostration retreat in the fall. After I was done, I went for my second winter *Kyol Che* and then to my solitary retreat in the mountains where I got the chickenpox.

I had a breakthrough in my prostration practice during the first winter *Kyol Che* practice, which I described in the chapter titled "Tigers and Pussycats." In the beginning, I hated doing the 108 prostrations in twenty minutes, which were required the first thing in the morning. I hated the manic, relentless pace of them. Then something happened that shifted my attitude and changed the experience. Toward the end of the ninety days, I stopped thinking about when it was going to end, when I would be free from the doing the prostrations at such a breakneck pace. I relaxed. The speed of the prostrations ceased to bother me. I surrendered to the flow and just did them. I stopped fighting and questioning and resisting.

The sweat ran down my face and pooled on the floor in front of me in the freezing Chan

Hall. I could hear myself panting. My heart was pumping. But my mind was quiet and peaceful. Clear. Calm. Bright.

As with so much in Korea, the retreat took its toll on my body. My joints now are very loose, like rubber bands. They flop this way and that, and I am still being treated by various doctors for this condition.

32

The Cool and Gentle Ointment of Chan

When people have problems or stress, they often try to forget whatever is pressing on them and put it out of their minds. They exercise, go to a spa, sing karaoke, drink, and drug themselves into oblivion or dance the night away. They go shopping. They buy, buy, buy. That is their therapy. Others eat—chocolate, potato chips. They turn on the television and watch and watch. Some people sleep and keep on sleeping.

These strategies provide instant gratification, a sudden release. It is as if you are itchy and you need to scratch that itch, but the more you scratch the more you itch.

Buy, buy, buy!

Eat, eat, eat!

You still feel empty and shallow.

After the high, you drop into a void.

The band packs up. The music stops. The party's over.

Chan sees living as an art. We need to skillfully manage our lives. That's why in Chan we talk about skillful means, a kind of dexterity and cleverness.

In Chan, we teach in a nonconventional manner. We teach by going beyond books or any kind of standard procedure. We try to see the particular needs of each individual. We tailor our teaching to the person, to each individual's dimensions, who the person is and where he or she is at in that very moment of life.

Come back to your breath. Come back to the present moment. Relax.

You have an itch?

Soothe it with the cool and gentle ointment of Chan.

33

FULLY ENGAGED

I AM OFTEN asked whether Chan will make you a better person. Well, it depends. Chan is a sharp knife. It can cut vegetables or it can be used to harm or kill. The refined, trained mind, if not properly used, can be dangerous. Some people can develop what we call "Chan sickness."

As you practice, your focus sharpens; you become steadier and gain confidence. You can see things that other people may not see. You can become arrogant, impatient, and egotistical. People with this kind of Chan sickness criticize and condemn.

This is a trend in Buddhism today. Compared to the past, lay practitioners have more opportunity to practice. They pick up some knowledge of Buddhism and become proud.

Knowing is one thing. Being able to truly attain and to do is another.

Arrogance is one form of Chan sickness. Another is a kind of frustration and withdrawal from the world. Chan practitioners with this condition can become easily angered and impatient. During meditation they feel the body and breath. They go into an absorbed state and become peaceful and happy. When they stop meditating, however, they are overwhelmed by the chaos of the world and all its problems. They become frightened and want to run away.

There are laypeople who come to my meditation retreats and they feel wonderful. But they don't want to become monastics because the monastic life is full of restrictions—no meat, sex, alcohol, television, or gambling. Yet they also don't want to go back into society, which they now perceive as overly stressful and busy. They do part-time work so that any chance they get they can escape on retreat. They live a kind of dangling life: They are not really laypeople, but they are also not monastics. They are half and half.

When you practice Chan, you don't withdraw. Chan is about the here and now. It's about being fully engaged in daily life. Chan and life are not separate: They are one and the same. Chan is not about meditating all the time, saying mantras, or doing prostrations so you don't have time for cooking, cleaning the house, developing your career, or looking after you children.

In Chan, you fully engage in life and learn to take on more responsibility. You have a bigger heart, a bigger mind. You do not stand on the sidelines, pointing out other people's mistakes and failures. You do not criticize, condemn, or carp. You treat people with respect. You lift people up. You practice kindness and compassion. You practice forgiveness. You find the good in people. You see the Buddha that is inside all of us, and you help others to see it too.

34

CHAN AND ART

IN CHAN WE talk about "skillful means." Chan can be deeply philosophical or transparently simple. It is often said to be the teaching of no-words. It breaks through conceptualizations. It precedes and supercedes doctrine.

It was in this spirit that Chan embraced art, especially as laypeople began coming to the monasteries and interacting with monastics. Art became a way to teach, to show the nature of Chan and probe its essence. Chan arts like calligraphy, tea, or poetry are a bridge between secular society and the religious life of the monasteries.

Even in the Mahayana tradition, which devotes itself to saving all sentient beings, the monks in Chan monasteries often had a tendency to focus wholly on self-liberation at the expense of reaching out and trying to help others. Chan art reached into the secular world, and it also was a way the secular world reached into the monasteries and influenced them.

From my point of view as a teacher of Chan, art is a skillful means of helping laypeople benefit from what Chan has to offer. I often teach groups of people who are coming into retreats from the outside world, with all its stresses and problems. Their minds are distracted and cloudy in a way that we don't experience as monastics in a monastery setting. In the monastery, there is basically no stress. The routine is fixed. One is enclosed and cloistered. The upshot is that when you sit down to meditate it's easy to be focused. There is no interference.

The qualities of Chan that influenced art and were expressed in what could be called the Chan aesthetic were simplicity, directness, and a feeling of aliveness or spontaneity. There was also an attempt to see something as it is, to express its original nature, its original face, to see into the truth of things, which is just another way of recognizing and expressing beauty.

Even the martial arts were shaped by Chan. Bodhidharma, according to tradition, directly contributed to the development of the martial arts of the famous Shaolin monastery. Because of long hours of meditation, he developed certain exercises for strengthening the muscles and tendons, which were documented in the *Yi Jin Jing*, a text ascribed to him, that is a classic of *chi kung* literature and practice.

In Chan art, we see a seamless merging of Buddhism and Chinese culture. I'm learning to play the flute and also learning calligraphy and painting and tea ceremony because I think we need to bring all of these practices and occupations into Buddhism.

Chan Buddhism is very lively.

Chan has no form. And as a result it has many, many forms.

Chan has no method, and as a result, it has innumerable methods.

This is the spirit of Chan:

To be alive. To adapt. To change.

This is also the creative spirit and its expression in art.

35

CHAN AND SEX

THE FIRST MONASTIC precept is to abstain from any sexual activity, even masturbation or watching pornography. We want to channel our sexual energy in other directions—to help other people, for example.

Family life can be a distraction for meditative activities and transcendental pursuits. Households and spouses and children, as my lay disciples are quick to confirm, take a tremendous lot of work. And on the spiritual path, sexual desire can be distracting, especially if the mind is always on sex.

Biologically, the male sexual organ is hot because of an increase in blood flow. Western medicine now offers Viagra for just this purpose—to increase blood flow. In certain Taoist practices, the same result can be achieved by pumping *chi* instead of pumping blood. In some Buddhist, Taoist, and Hindu sects, pumping *chi* leads to a practice of what we call a unification of man and woman. Man and woman come together as a spiritual practice.

The Chan view is that these practices developed because of an abundance of sexual energy. The initiates had too much energy and didn't know what to do with it. It had to go somewhere! These practices need to be approached with caution. If you have too much desire, in the end it will burn you.

If you feel that you have very strong sexual desire or have a problem with your sexual energy, bring your awareness and attention to your *yong quan*, the center of the sole of your foot. Bringing your attention there will help regulate your desire. Chinese acupuncture uses this point to help people with extreme sexual energy (rapists, for example).

You cannot expect everyone to be saints. There are human needs. Chan accepts the imperfection of the world. Chan is practical. For a layperson, some sexual activity is permitted. You are not part of a monastic order. Chan advises you to practice in moderation. So how moderate is moderate? You have to find that out for yourself.

36

STRAIGHT FOUNDATION,
SHARP AX

IN CHAN, WE start with particular practices of sitting and breathing, master them, and develop strong concentration. We try to set a straight foundation, otherwise the structure we build will be wobbly and precarious.

There is a story in the Sutra of One Hundred Parables, which is called Bai Yu Jing in Chinese. One day, a very wealthy merchant went to the city and saw a beautiful house. Back in his home he kept thinking about the house day and night. Finally, he asked an architect to accompany him to the city to look at it.

"Can you build me a house like that?" he asked the architect.

"No problem," the architect replied.

"Go, do it," said merchant.

He went back to his village a happy man. He bought a special plot of land for his home-to-be and went each day to visit the construction site.

The first day, he didn't see anything; the second, third, and fourth days there was nothing as well. A week went by and he saw absolutely no progress on his new home.

He summoned the architect.

"We have to sketch the building. And then order material," the architect explained.

The merchant waited. Still no building. He summoned the architect.

"We have to lay the foundation," the architect said. "We need to pour cement and lay the foundation slowly. We need to make sure the foundation is straight. Then we'll build the first, second, and third floors."

"Let's dispense with all that," said the merchant. "It's the third floor I really like, with its sloping roof and lovely balcony. I only want the third floor."

So it is with our practice. We can't just have the third floor. It seems obvious, but it pays to remember in whatever we set out to do that all great accomplishments start from the basics, from the foundation.

In another version of the story, the architect built the third floor. The merchant returned from the business trip all anticipation. As he approached the house site, he could see the beautiful third floor rising above the trees. But when he came to house he found the architect had built the third floor on pillars and he couldn't get up!

The biggest trees need the deepest, widest roots. Their roots are at least the width of the tree's canopy.

How deep should your roots be? How wide? I can't tell you. You need to find out for yourself.

In Chan, we not only talk about how the tree grows, we also talk about chopping it down. It's most important that the ax is sharp. You can spend a lot of time hacking away with a blunt ax without result.

There is a story of three woodcutters. The first immediately started chopping the tree. The second sharpened his ax for a short time and then began to chop. The third spent a lot of time sharpening the ax.

In the beginning, the first two cutters laughed at the third. But then he started chopping and by lunch he had finished the job. He went home carrying his load. Now he was the one laughing.

Spend time sharpening the ax. Sit over the sharpening stone and rub the blade against it. Hone and hone. When you're ready go to cut, your effort won't be wasted. You won't need to use much force. You can work quickly and cleanly. The blade will do the work.

In whatever you hope to accomplish, set a straight foundation. Sharpen your ax.

37

How We Treat Others

CHAN MUST EXPRESS itself in the way we treat each other or it is useless. I have people who come to learn with me who are well versed in Buddhism. They know their dharma. They have studied with Mahayana, Theravada, and Vajrayana teachers. They can chant sutras. They come to the monastery or on retreat and bow and speak gently, but when they return home, they scold and shout and scream.

What good is all their Buddhist learning?

It is only by changing the way we treat others that we can hope to change the world and make it a kinder, more peaceful, compassionate, and hopeful place. We can help change others by touching them with gentleness, kindness, and forgiveness. But before we can do that, first we must touch ourselves in this way. We need to begin our own inner transformation.

38

SEE FOR YOURSELF

WE CAN BE so easily fooled by appearances. I look around. My eyes see the room I'm sitting in. Is the room real? My eyes tell me it is, that it is real and solid. But when I take away its pieces—the beams, the timber, the walls—it doesn't exist. Does that mean the room is also unreal? No. It is also not unreal.

Chan teaches us that we shouldn't fall too far into either extreme—existing or not existing. Our consciousness should not become fixed or attached to the way things seem to be.

There is a story of a turtle and a fish. They were very good friends and lived in the middle of a big ocean. Each day they went together for a coffee break and had a nice chat.

Then one day the fish didn't see the turtle. Where is the turtle, he wondered? It was very odd. After about a week, the turtle returned.

"Why haven't I seen you this past week?" said the fish.

"I went on holiday," said the turtle.

"Where did you go?"

"A place called land."

"What was it like? Please describe it to me."

"There is no water and there were people everywhere, walking around on two legs instead of swimming!"

The fish was flabbergasted. "I don't believe it!" he exclaimed. "How can there be a land with no water? And how can these things called 'people' walk on two legs?"

The fish couldn't conceive of land because he was attached to his consciousness—the aggregate of thoughts, emotions, perceptions, memories, everything that is going on in his mind. But in Chan we shouldn't deny experiences we have not had for ourselves.

Chan is all about experience. People try to use their intelligence and knowledge to find out what meditation is all about. But a fish cannot experience dry land.

Always have an open heart and mind. Try for yourself. Your own experience is the best—really the only—teacher.

This is the message of the Kalama Sutra. Buddha came to the village of Kalama. The villagers asked: "Why should we listen to what you have to say. Lots of teachers and sages come through here and tell us they have some special insight into reality or they've found the ultimate truth."

To which the Buddha replied: "Do not follow my teachings because it's tradition or because some outside authority says that's what you should do. Neither follow what I have to say because everyone is doing it or because you have heard that it's beneficial. You should have your own experience and then decide."

This is Buddha's teaching of *Ehipassiko*, which literally means "come and see for yourself."

39

BUDDHA NATURE

I HAVE TRAVELED widely in Asia and Europe, spent three years in the West at Master Sheng Yen's retreat center in Pine Bush, New York, and four years in Australia. I have come to feel that the hearts and minds of all the people in all our different countries and cultures are more or less the same.

We Chinese talk about love and respect for our parents and elders. But this kind of love and respect is not only Chinese. Whether you are black, white, or yellow—we all love and respect our parents and grandparents. We also all love our children. We look after them and bring them up. We are not as different as we sometimes like to think. Our basic humanness—the way we think and feel—is similar.

"I love you," we say in English. In Chinese, we say, *Wo ai ni*. Koreans say, *Sarang hae yo*; Japanese, *Aishiteru*; Indonesians, *Aku cinta kamu*; Filipinos, *Mahal kita*; and Vietnamese, *Anh yêu em*.

How many different ways there are of saying "I love you"! How many different ways can I say it? So many. And yet the feeling is the same. The meaning is the same.

Love doesn't change. And so it is with the basic problems of the mind: greed, anger, desire, and craving. Unhappiness in human beings, all our negative emotions, are the same. There is no difference between Indian anger, Chinese anger, and American anger. They are identical.

There is a wonderful story from Chan that illustrates this. The sixth lineage master, Huineng, who remained illiterate throughout his life, had an awakening upon hearing a recitation of part of the Diamond Sutra. He traveled from his home in Guangdong to seek out the fifth lineage master, Hongren, in his monastery on Huangmei Mountain. Hongren tested him. It was like a battle!

"Where are you from?" Hongren asked. He was asking, "What is your original nature?" He was testing his depth.

"The south," Huineng replied. He was waiting, giving the relative answer first. He did not jump right to the absolute.

"People from the south are barbaric," said Hongren (to call someone a barbarian is the ultimate insult in China). Hongren was testing, probing, pushing in.

"North, south; all people have buddha nature," Huineng calmly replied.

"Go to the kitchen and pound rice," said Hongren, satisfied with the answer, but perhaps thinking that Huineng was a bit of an intellectual, a smart aleck—hence, the rice pounding. It is very Chan to distrust the intellect and glib answers. The emphasis is on direct experience and hard work.

That was the end of the first exchange and the first teaching. Huineng was a small man and the rice pounder was quite heavy; he tied rocks around his waist to give him ballast.

North, south—all people have buddha nature.

Huineng is saying that underneath our vexations we are all Buddhas—loving, compassionate, awakened beings. Chan is about discovering that love inside us and seeing it in others. To see buddha nature in all of us. That is the essence of Chan.

Although Chan is Chinese, it applies to all human beings. Everyone can come back to the present moment. And everyone is equal. Everyone has exactly the same opportunity to learn Chan and realize his or her buddha nature. Chinese, Indians, Americans, rich, poor, in between—it doesn't matter.

"I love you!"

No matter the language, the meaning is always the same.

40

BLIND CAT, DEAD MOUSE

OUR SENSES ARE prone to the imaginative, hallucinatory, or illusionary. Sometimes in meditation you hear a cricket or an ant crawling in the grass. Or you hear people talking far away in the kitchen. You can hear their conversation word for word. After meditation, you go down to the kitchen and repeat what they've said. They are flabbergasted. How could you have possibly heard what they were saying? They think you must have superpowers.

Or you're sitting. Suddenly you know what everyone in the room is thinking. Or you know what's happening at home. Or you suddenly know what is going to happen tomorrow. You have a vision: Jimmy is falling down the stairs. Then tomorrow comes and what happens? Jimmy falls down the stairs! You think you have ESP. A sixth sense.

What is the reason for your wonderful newfound powers? During meditation your mind becomes clear and your senses sharpen.

Some people who practice meditation get caught in a quest for these seemingly supernatural abilities. Their senses become sharper, and they are able to stay in this state. They can have uncanny insight or perception. They can tell the future or read your thoughts. I have, on occasion, been accused of possessing such powers.

One of my students brought a *chi kung* master renowned for what's called "third-eye vision" to my monastery. He carefully inspected me and told my student that there was light coming from my forehead, and it was very bright.

"Then why do I still need to turn on the light when I go into a dark room at night?" I asked.

Another *chi kung* master said I must have very high wisdom because he could see lots of little lotuses growing out of the top of my head.

"Then I must have *chou tuo*," I quipped. This is a Chinese affliction that means "smelly head."

Once a woman who was a *chi kung* practitioner and wife of a *chi kung* master brought her beads for me to bless. I don't really know how to bless beads or anything else, for that matter. People ask me for my blessings all the time, and I do hope they work, otherwise I'm afraid they won't contribute money to help rebuild my monastery!

This woman seemed sincere, so I thought I might as well give it a shot and do something to make her happy. The beads were around her neck, and she bent forward reverentially. I took the beads in my hands and started muttering the first thing that came into my head—prayers to Kuan Yin. Immediately she jumped back in a great leap that must have been two or three meters. She landed like a panther and went into very impressive kung fu pose.

"Oh, *Shifu*," she cried, using my honorific title in Chinese, which means "father-teacher." "Your *chi* is so strong!"

I had to laugh to myself.

IN CHINESE WE have a saying: "The blind cat caught a dead mouse." If you get caught up in such supernatural exploits, in the end you became a fool. The purpose of Chan is not to achieve supernatural or extrasensory power.

What if it is not only you but everyone in the room who experiences supernatural phenomena? On my meditation retreats, people often report a light shining from between the eyebrows of the statue of the Buddha on the altar of the Chan Hall where they meditate. They respectfully wish to know if the light is real.

"Treat it as if it is a dream, something illusionary," I say. "Reflect on the words of the Diamond Sutra: '*Fan so you siang cie se xi huan*. All phenomena are like a dream, illusionary, a mirage.' Return to your breath."

They ask me if illusionary experiences are the work of the demon Mara, who in Buddhism is the rough equivalent of Satan or the devil. Mara, as happened with Buddha himself, appears when people are on the brink of enlightenment and tries to trap them, luring them back into *samsara*, the endless cycle of birth and death.

"Don't worry," I tell my students. "Mara usually appears to only very advanced practitioners. Mara will look at us and say, 'I can't be bothered!'"

It can help to realize that all these demons come from our hearts and minds. From our greed, hatred, ignorance, and craving. From desire, lust, and anger. These qualities may resonate with something that is external—an energy outside of us to which we have an affinity. I don't want to make it sound like the movie *Ghostbusters*. Most likely, what appear to be demons are actually manifestations of something within us.

A STORY ILLUSTRATES Chan's take on the supernatural. There was a monk who was a very diligent meditator. He practiced morning, afternoon, and night. During his nighttime meditations, something very strange began to happen. He saw a giant spider coming down from the ceiling. It was bigger around than a large pizza! *Shuiih, shuiih, shuiih.* It dropped down on its sticky, silken thread. It dropped closer and closer to him, all the while sharpening its teeth and claws.

This happened every night when he meditated. He became a bit disturbed. What should I do, he wondered? He went to see his master and confided: "Each night, whenever I start to meditate, I see a monstrous spider coming down. And this spider is sharpening its claws and teeth as if it's going to eat me!"

"What do you want to do?" the master asked.

"I'm going to get a knife. And, tonight, when I see the spider, I'll pretend I'm meditating. Because whenever I open up my eyes and look up at him he disappears. So tonight I'll pretend I'm meditating and hide the knife behind me. And when the spider comes near, I'm going to poke him in the stomach and kill him!"

"Don't use a knife," the master said and gave the monk a calligraphy brush.

"This is a magic brush," the master said. "And this is magic ink. When the spider comes, pretend to be meditating, and then bring the brush out and draw a circle on the stomach of the spider, and then the spider will disappear."

That night the monk did as his master suggested. Pretending to meditate, he soon heard the sound of the spider descending. *Shuiih, shuiih, shuiih.* He sensed the spider drawing near, so he glanced up and whipped out his brush. The spider was right in front of him. In a flash, he drew a circle on the spider's belly. Immediately, the spider disappeared.

The next morning, the monk was very happy. He went to see his master.

"Tell me what happened," the master said.

"It was just as you said. I pretended to meditate and the spider came for me. I took the brush you gave me, quickly drew a circle on his stomach, and he disappeared!"

"Come forward," said the master.

The monk walked over and the master pulled up his shirt. There, on the master's belly, was a circle of ink. The monk was startled. Then the master pulled up the monk's shirt. On the monk's stomach there was a circle as well.

"It seems we caught two big spiders!" the master said. "I'm so glad you didn't use a knife to poke me in the belly."

WHAT IS THE lesson of this story? When strange phenomena happen, don't be distracted. Don't let them preoccupy you or run your mind. Let them go. Keep returning to the present moment and your breath. The present moment is what is real. The rest is illusionary. Relax and breathe. Don't give your attention to spiders sharpening their teeth and claws. Don't be a blind cat with a dead mouse.

41

Sleeping Buddha

When you meditate consistently, you notice that you sleep less. Usually when I'm on retreat, I sleep about four hours. It's enough, and I don't feel tired during the day. Why? Because the body has enough rest when the mind is not becoming exhausted all the time with wandering and scattered thoughts.

This kind of disjointed mental activity has a depleting effect on our energy. What happens when the mind is moving back into the past, into the future, grasping and rejecting, judging and discriminating, trying to obtain pleasure and avoid pain, trying to convince itself that impermanence does not exist and the self will live on in comfort and glory forever? You tell me.

On a basic level, you burn up energy. All those neurons firing and firing, communicating back and forth, up and down, every which way. Many thoughts come with somatic reactions, which are both subtle and not so subtle. The body tenses. All this burns energy in ways that are quite perceptible when you regularly meditate. The somatic results of cognitive action are apparent, as is the toll of the way we're always trying to do a kind of psychological balancing act; always trying to come back into harmony, resolve contradictions, and make everything all right.

When you're doing meditation properly, it's much more relaxing than sleeping. Dreaming can be tiring, and sleeping itself can be light or deep with less REM activity and concurrent somatic results.

Some accomplished meditators don't lie down to sleep. Sitting is able to sustain the body. As your practice goes deeper, you require less and less sleep. You come to a point where you can just sit up. It's enough: you feel as though you don't need any sleep. But this should be developed naturally. Others try this practice, but it is not for them, and they damage their spines.

As you meditate and sleep less, the quality of your sleep improves. You sleep more deeply. And when you're sleeping, you feel more peaceful and stable. You can even meditate as you sleep. We call this "sleeping yoga."

This involves actually bringing your awareness into sleep. For example, I was once on retreat with Master Sheng Yen in Pine Bush. After we were through meditating for the day, I went back to my room and lay down. I assumed the auspicious posture, common in Theravada tradition, of the sleeping Buddha. I reclined on my right side, with my legs one on top of the other and tucked up a little bit. This posture is good for sleep. You're not pressing your heart by lying on your left side or your spine while lying on your back. If you snore, it is also a good posture and can help reduce the sound.

I was counting my breath, a form of meditation practice. I relaxed my whole body and counted my breath: one, two . . . and then three. But I had a strange feeling and looked at the clock. Five hours had passed between the counts of two and three!

Those five hours passed in an instant. It wasn't normal sleep where the mind grows dark. My mind was clear and light, as if I were still meditating. I slept from about 10:30 pm to 3:30 am. Tok, tok, tok went the sound of the wood "waking" board at four.

That day, I told Master Sheng Yen about taking the auspicious posture and the experience that followed. He just smiled.

"You had a good sleep," he said.

42

TRUE LOVE

MOST OF THE love we have is possessive: it's about the self. That is not true love; it is self-love. When you see someone who attracts you that feeling is not about the person. We like the person because we have a good feeling inside of us when he or she is around. The good feeling is all about us. As a result, we want to possess that person. But what we really want is the good feeling—not the person! It is an important distinction.

If love is only about the self, then this relationship will not last. Maybe you feel stale or bored. The initial excitement and infatuation wears off. When the person can no longer give you that good feeling, what do you do? You change partners.

If we are able to start relationships with friendliness and loving-kindness, love will develop. You will feel a sense of closeness, a softness and tenderness. That is when we truly open up. We are able to embrace and accommodate. We become more understanding and accepting. This love is a form of kindness. It is not only about caring, protecting, giving—there is also in it forgiveness and acceptance. You accept the person whole. You see their strengths and weaknesses. You relax. Then you are able to open your heart and mind and accept them.

That is a true love.

43

Enlightenment
Will Get You

The taste of liberation is the taste of Chan.

Where does liberation come from? It comes from cleaning the cup, from freeing oneself from ignorance and the vexations of craving, greed, and anger. In this way we become liberated from harmful behaviors and actions.

Liberation also comes when you attain the state of absorption. The elephant walking. The clear, calm steadiness of mind.

Attaining wisdom is liberation. For Buddhists this is liberation from *samsara*—the endless cycle of birth and death.

From the perspective of Chan, buddha nature is always within. Chan is a method of simply opening up. We sometimes refer to this inner buddha as the Muni pearl because the Buddha's name is Shakyamuni. *Muni* means "a precious pearl." We sometimes call it the wish-fulfilling pearl. When the mind starts to open up, the pearl of buddha nature is revealed.

That is why we can think of liberation as no-vow, no-motivation, no-practice. We call this *wu yen* in Chinese, which means "not-vow." In this case, *yen* means not wishing, not aspiring, not achieving. The vow has become you. It has internalized in you and become your nature. And yet in Buddhism the vows we take to practice, to deliver sentient beings, to keep the precepts are so important. They provide motivation and direction. Liberation is like coming home; there is no need for motivation and direction. You are home. You relax, you rest, you feel completely yourself. You are at ease and peaceful.

When you see your real nature, buddha nature is already there. You do not need to add or remove anything. There is no need to practice, no need for vows or intentions. You've been trying and trying and actually everything you've been looking for has been right under your nose all the time! You just hadn't realized it was there.

Chan Master Hanshan went to the toilet in the middle of the night. The door slammed right into the front of his face. At that moment he became awakened. He exclaimed: "Oh, the nose actually points downward!"

Try not to misunderstand. Please don't think, "I'm already the Buddha, so why do I need to practice?" You go around doing what you want. We call people who behave in this way the crazy Buddha. The ignorant Buddha. The sleeping Buddha. The greedy Buddha. The unawakened Buddha. In other words, sentient beings. It is the awakened sentient being that is called the Buddha.

The annals of Buddhism and the sutras generally highlight the moment of enlightenment, not the long and arduous sort of practice that preceded that moment. We rarely see how much effort the masters who became enlightened put into their practice.

I am often asked whether after they become enlightened Chan masters still practice. If you become enlightened, I will give you these instructions: Practice like you did before your enlightenment. When you awaken, everything becomes clear. But then it all becomes dark again.

Before enlightenment and after enlightenment there are different stages of practice. And there are different degrees of enlightenment or awakening. We can have a mini enlightenment, great enlightenment, or even complete enlightenment. And there are no guarantees. Enlightenment can happen at any time or not at all.

Master Xu Yun, Empty Cloud, who was born in Guangzhou, practiced diligently for many years but there was no experience, nothing, no news. He wandered around China. Then at the age of fifty-six, he was drinking tea. Scalding tea spilled onto his hand. He let go of the cup, and it dropped and shattered on the floor. At that moment he became awakened. His verses commemorating the event are very beautiful in Chinese:

> *The vast space of emptiness shatters*
> *And the great earth falls into place.*

Another great Chan master, Zhaozhou, was still wandering at the age of eighty-four. When asked by his disciple for instruction, Zhaozhou asked: "Have you had your breakfast?"

"No," said the disciple.

"Go eat breakfast," Zhaozhou replied.

Another disciple came to Zhaozhou. "What is your practice, Master?" he asked.

"Have you had your breakfast?"

"Yes," said the disciple.

"Have you washed your bowl?"

"No."

"Go wash your bowl," said Zhaozhou.

Another disciple came to Zhaozhou.

"Have you eaten breakfast?"

"Yes," the disciple replied.

"Have you cleaned your bowl?"

"Yes."

"Go drink tea."

WHEN TALKING ABOUT enlightenment in Chan we use the metaphor of a dam. The dam collects water behind it. If the dam is shallow, it collects water quickly. If it's a big dam, it may take a long time for the water to collect. When that dam becomes full, the moment you open it up the water gushes out and you are able to generate an enormous amount of energy.

Enlightenment is like this. Sometimes we quickly have an experience of awakening. It may be shallow or deep, this or that. So don't bother about it. Don't trouble yourself about the different stages of absorption or the levels of enlightenment. Just keep practicing. That is, in fact, enlightenment. Chan masters can experience awakening again and again. One Chan master said he had a great awakening over thirty times and countless small awakenings. So awakening is not something that occurs and then is finished. The fog parts and you see the mountaintop. That is your destination. The fog closes back in. You keep walking. You are very sure because you clearly see the path, even in the fog. You continue your journey.

Chan is different from other types of Buddhism in this way. Other Buddhist schools say keep walking in the fog. You have faith that eventually you will get to mountain even though you haven't seen it. Eventually you will get there. Chan gives you a sudden glimpse of the shining peak in the moment when the fog clears. Still, you need to keep walking. Still, you have to climb the mountain.

People think that when you become enlightened, you're Buddha, and your job is done. If only it were so.

How can we tell whether enlightenment has occurred? When does a teacher test a disciple? Does the student say, "I'm prepared, now you can test me?" No, the teacher usually tests the disciple when the disciple least expects it. This is when state of mind is most natural, in its original state. In those moments, we say the spark of fire ignites, the fireworks go off.

Chan masters do not say, "I have a feeling I'm going to be enlightened soon. Enlightenment is close!" There's no such thing. All Chan masters became awakened and enlightened when they least expected it.

Chan masters don't think about enlightenment; they don't think about awakening; they only think about practice, practice, and practice. As a result, they never expect enlightenment, and then enlightenment comes. If you just keep practicing, and you do not grasp at enlightenment or run away from it, enlightenment will get you.

All the Chan masters only want to practice; they don't want to be enlightened or awakened. As a result, they become enlightened and awakened.

No Chan masters wanted to be Chan masters. And as a result, they became masters of Chan.

44

SWEET POTATO

As was recorded in the Precepts for Monastics, the disciples asked Buddha for instruction on cleaning the toilet.

"Buddha, we see insects in the toilet. What should we do?"

"Clean the toilet," the Buddha replied.

The disciples went back and began cleaning, but some of the parts of the toilet still had insects on them.

"Buddha, when we cleaned the toilet, the insects didn't go away. What do we do?"

"Clean the toilet," the Buddha said.

The disciples went back and started cleaning again. This time they couldn't help killing some insects.

Again, they went to the Buddha.

"The insects died, what should we do?"

"Clean the toilet."

MAHAYANA BUDDHISM is always about intention and motivation. It's about the spirit behind our actions. If you're cleaning the toilet and your precepts are telling you that you can't kill the cockroaches, but in your heart you want to kill them, that's not healthy.

Consider the following situation.

One day you're sitting peacefully under a tree on lovely summer's day. A rabbit comes running by, darting this way and that. It turns for a moment and looks at you, then runs away to your left into the forest.

A minute later a hunter appears.

"Have you seen a rabbit?" the hunter asks. "Which way did it go?"

What would your answer be?

If you are a monk, you are in a bind. Your precepts forbid you from killing, but they also forbid you from lying. If you tell the truth and say "left," the rabbit may die. If you keep silent, the rabbit has a fifty-fifty chance; still, it could be argued that if the hunter kills the rabbit you're responsible. After all, passivity is no excuse. If you lie and tell the hunter "right," you're breaking your precepts. You also have to consider that the hunter may have a family that will go hungry tonight if he can't kill the rabbit. He needs to eat. So what to do?

The Chan spirit is to ask the hunter to sit down and have tea. You ask about his life and his family. Does he have any children? How many?

Is his home far? His father and mother? Are they living? You have a nice conversation and share a few laughs. And when he's ready to start hunting again, you give him a sweet potato.

45

Our Birthright

When our lives are not in harmony we experience stress, pressure, and tension. There is an imbalance. As a result, there is conflict. This is *duhkha*, a Sanskrit word that is central to Buddhism and usually translated as "suffering."

In fact, *duhkha* has many different levels of meaning. In a basic sense, it simply means "out of place." The Buddha says *duhkha* is like a wheel out of joint: it can't rotate on its axle. The wheel whines and complains as it turns. So, similarly, in our life, when we feel out of place, we experience dissonance, whether in body, mind, body and mind, the self and others, or the self and the world.

Duhkha can also mean "entrapped." Sometimes we are trapped in our emotions, or in what feels like an impossible situation or relationship. We are overwhelmed and feel helpless and overpowered.

All these conditions cause us to feel out of tune. This could also be thought of as a kind of disconnection or alienation. We're out of position.

There is friction. Our lives are not moving well. It is this position of entanglement that Chan addresses. Chan is about freeing oneself, although freedom does not mean an abnegation of social responsibilities or obligations. The freedom of Chan is the freedom of fish in the ocean or birds in the sky. There may be obstructions in our path, but we gracefully fly or swim around them. We have the wisdom to see them in advance and avoid them and the clarity of vision to see our destination.

In the Chinese Sutra of Golden Radiance there is a story of the four snakes, which appears in the chaper "Emptiness." A man fell down into a deep well. At the bottom of the well were four poisonous snakes, two dark in color, two light. The snakes represent our four elements. The light snakes are water and wind; the dark, earth and fire. These snakes are constantly waiting to devour us.

The man quickly climbs up the well's rope, away from the snakes. But rats are chewing on the rope. The rats represent impermanence. As the man climbs, he sees a honeycomb on the well's wall. He forgets the snakes and the rats, distracted by his desire for the honey. The bees may sting him— still, he reaches out for the honey with his hand . . .

This is how we go through life, grabbing for the honey, getting stung by bees, while we blot out the rats and snakes from our minds.

Buddhism talks about the causes of suffering.

We suffer during birth, the aches and pains of old age. We suffer during sickness, when we die, and when we grieve the death of people we care about. We suffer when we don't get what we want, and when we try to hold on to it once we have it.

Buddhism has sophisticated spiritual mechanisms and philosophical insights for treating suffering, but these techniques are largely geared toward monastics living in a monastic community who lead contemplative and rather sheltered lives. What about the vast majority of people who live in the world and have families and jobs? I would like to reframe suffering for them as something that's less pervasive and fundamental than it is usually made out to be in Buddhism. The emphasis on suffering in Buddhism can be overwhelming. But I would insist that Buddhism is about the freedom we talked about earlier. The Buddha's emphasis was on living.

Duhkha is that which keeps us from feeling fully alive. From the vitality and joy of life that is our birthright.

What should we do? Rest the body and mind from wandering and scattered thoughts. Do not engage with hurtful impulses and emotions. The more we are able to relax, the more our minds will rest. We will be able to rest our bodies and minds in the present moment.

46

A Taste
Like the Ocean

1

WHAT IS CHAN?

Chan is a happy life with wisdom and compassion.

To learn Chan is to learn to be happy, to learn to lead a happy life.

What are wisdom and compassion?

I cannot tell you.

You have to experience them for yourself.

2

CHAN IS NOT the formal teaching of what is called the *buddhadharma*, which in this case refers to the terminology of Buddhism, the book learning and formal corpus of Buddhist knowledge. The teachings of Chan are called *Xinfa* in Chinese—the teaching of heart and mind. In Chan, we open our hearts and minds to our loved ones and then to the whole world.

In Chinese we have a saying that approximates the Golden Rule: "If you do not wish it to happen to you, do not do it to others." Isn't it wonderful that East and West came up with the same basic thought about the way people should treat each other?

In the West, the Golden Rule is a basis of moral behavior that, if followed, helps people live together in peace and harmony. But in Chan it is not only this. There is more to it. We see no separation between me and you, us and them. We are all the same. The interconnection between all of us and the entire universe, in fact, is not speculative or theoretical. It is experiential and exists in every breath we take, in every moment we share on this great earth.

An expression of this in Chan is the *sagara mudra*, otherwise known as the oceanic *mudra*, a form of *samadhi*. Everything flows into the ocean. The ocean accommodates the big and small, the whales and prawns. We sometimes think of the waves and water as different. Big waves look down at small waves. Small waves feel inferior to waves that are big. Yet when the ocean calms and becomes tranquil and flat, where is the difference in the size of the waves?

We all have the same buddha nature. All the teachings are the same. They all have one taste like the ocean. The taste of salt.

The Chan experience is to realize that the happiness of the self is dependent on the happiness of others. In Chinese we say, "Buddhas of the ten directions breathe through the same nostril." We all breathe together.

This is a very Chinese idea: the strong, tight sense of family, the strong interconnection between all levels of society. But in Chan, the hierarchies, so much a part of the Confucian model, are dispensed with. We are all equal. We not only treat others as we would have them treat us. We are others. There is no difference. No separation.

This is the insight behind what we call the Four Immeasurables, the way in Chan we aspire to treat others. The first immeasurable is *metta*, loving-kindness, the genuine wish that I may be well as you may be well. The second is *karuna*, to remove suffering: When I see you suffering, I will make you well. The third is *mudita*: The joy at your happiness is my joy, and there is no envy in it, no regret; we rejoice in each other's merits. The fourth immeasurable is *upeksha*, nonattachment: I remove your suffering, but I do not think I'm superior. This is the quality of equanimity.

3

WHAT IS BEAUTY in Chan? To see something fully, experience it fully, and become one with it.

4

We call Chan a lazy practice. You are lazy in Chan. Why? Because you stay with the method. You don't go out to wandering and scattered thoughts. You don't go into the past or the future. Thoughts say: "Come, come, come! Come out and play!" And you reply, "No, thank you. I'm too lazy!"

5

Chan, Zen, Son, and Thien are four brothers. Chan is Chinese; Zen, Japanese; Son, Korean; and Thien, Vietnamese.

Chan is the eldest brother.

Chan derives from the Sanskrit word *dhyana*, or "meditative states." But it is not about these meditative states of absorption but rather about wisdom. Zen, Son, and Thien are renditions of the word "Chan" in their various languages.

In Chan, you find masters who study, teach, and merge with other schools of Buddhism. But they are still, at their root, Chan masters. In all schools of Chinese Buddhism, you need to meditate. So you find the Chan spirit everywhere.

Chan is a Mahayana school of Buddhism, known as the larger vehicle. The practitioner of Chan is motivated by compassion, or *bodhicitta*. The Mahayana vow is to deliver all sentient beings, putting others before oneself.

This is the northern tradition of Buddhism as it

exists in Asia. The southern tradition is Theravada, which generally speaking took hold in Thailand, Laos, Burma, Cambodia, and Sri Lanka. The Buddhism that exists in Singapore, Malaysia, Indonesia, and the Philippines is a combination of Mahayana and Theravada. In the rest of the world, including America, we see a mix of Theravada and Mahayana.

6

BODHIDHARMA, ACCORDING TO some legends a Persian prince, is credited as the first lineage holder of Chan. According to most sources, he came to China in around 530 CE to teach "a special transmission outside scriptures, not founded in words and letters." Scholars disagree about whether he was an actual person or a composite.

I resonate with Bodhidharma for the strength of his practice. According to Chan legend, he spent nine years sitting in meditation in a cave. He was a traveler and went to a distant land where everything was strange and unfamiliar. I too have had that experience—more than once! Bodhidharma sat and sat and patiently waited for his teachings to take hold. I try to follow his example. Still, his approach is a bit too Indian for me, and he was a prince; my parents were simple people.

I have a special feeling for the sixth lineage holder, Huineng. He was a commoner like me and a woodcutter by trade. He was told by the fifth lineage master, Hongren: Go pound rice. That was his practice.

Huineng went into hiding because Hongren had given him transmission and verified his enlightenment experience. He gave him an alms bowl and a set of robes to signify his attainment. But he also told him to slip away in the middle of the night because Hongren's many other disciples were sure to be jealous and might not only try to strip Huineng of his bowl and robes but do away with him altogether because he was a painful reminder of their own lack of attainment.

Huineng left in the middle of the night and went to go live with the tribes, the hunters of the deep forests and the hills.

What I particularly love about Huineng is that his teachings are so direct and down-to-earth. He has a patience and gentleness that is very Chinese. He was so ordinary. So quiet. In his teachings, Chan finds its distinctively Chinese voice. It is adaptable, inclusive, all embracing, and accessible to common people. It is about daily living.

When I think of Huineng, I see him chopping wood and pounding rice.

47

My First Master

EVERYTHING HAS TWO sides, the good and the bad, the easy and hard, the pleasant and difficult. Chan has two sides as well. Chan masters will use a stick and hit you. They punch and shout. They can be really nasty. Why? They are testing you, testing your devotion and dedication.

I had my own form of this kind of training from my ordination master, Song Nian. His nuns could not hide their gloating when I became a monk. Now, as the youngest of his disciples, I would be his attendant. That terrible job no longer fell on them.

When I became a monk, I asked Song Nian: "When do I get my robes?"

He said, "That is your business, not mine. Go find them yourself."

Song Nian was in a Chan lineage, but he didn't teach. He had come to Singapore after fleeing Mainland China in 1949 when the Communists took over. He was from an aristocratic family and he feared for his life.

At birth, Song Nian didn't move or breathe. His mother gave him away to one of his sisters and wanted nothing more to do with him. He was sickly but precocious, and entered university at the young age of sixteen.

It was my job to take care of him. He was a tall man with a big build. When he was younger he had been a master of the martial arts. He was known for being handsome. He was a renowned calligrapher, and the combination of warrior and artist gave him a unique and compelling charisma. He was also a scholar, but scholars are not usually as physically strong and graceful as he was. He had long white eyebrows, and even at eighty-seven, his age when I first became his disciple, he always walked at a great pace. I had to run to keep up with him.

In his old age he had become enormously cantankerous. He would scold and scold and scold me from the first moment he saw me in the morning to when he closed his door each night in my face.

Every meal was one complaint after another, a litany of woes and gripes. I never served him the right amount of food.

On one day he would complain that his plate was too full.

"Are you trying to stuff me to death?" he would say. "Are you trying to bloat me and burst me with food?"

The next day I'd give him less.

"Guo Jun," he hissed. "Why do you give me so little?"

"Master, yesterday you said I gave you too much!"

"Seeds For Hell!" he barked, using my nickname and shaking his finger at me as if to curse. "Today, I am more active. I am hungry. I need more food!"

The breakfast of brown rice and bean porridge was never right. It was either too thick or thin. Because he was old and his teeth were bad, he couldn't chew. So the porridge couldn't be too thick. But if it was too thin, he'd hiss and point his finger: "Seeds For Hell, you are serving me soup!"

When we ate, I had to finish exactly one moment after him. If I was done eating before he was, he would scold me. "Why do you finish so fast? You are rushing me." If I finished after him, I was scolded. "Why are you so slow, Guo Jun? You always make me wait."

I had to help him around because he was frail. If I grabbed him too tightly to help him get up or walk, he'd shout at me. If I held him too lightly, he'd say I wanted him to fall and die. I had to walk just to his side and slightly behind him. When he turned his head slightly, I immediately had to be next to him, not too close and not too far. I had to anticipate his every wish.

If I walked too loudly, he scolded me for disturbing him. He would cock his head. "Did I hear a horse galloping?" he would say. Or: "Is there an elephant in the monastery?"

If I walked too softly, he called me a ghost and accused me of trying to frighten him by sneaking around. He would be startled. "Which hell are you from," he would hiss. "You are so quiet, like a snake."

He had a habit of peering at me with a kind of mock concern. "Guo Jun, you look older since the last time I saw you." It didn't matter if that had been two minutes before. "Why have you aged so much?" He would say this in a slithery, ominous tone. Was he trying to teach me impermanence? I still don't know. "Guo Jun, why do you look so old? Why have you aged?"

After he had an operation for gallstones, I had to sleep outside his room. He wouldn't hear of letting me sleep next to him on the floor. "I have treasures under my bed," he barked. "You're a thief and will steal them." He had a buzzer by his bed to summon me when he needed to go to the bathroom. If I delayed for an instant, he would wet his bed, and I would get hell from him. Because he was in a wheelchair, I had to shower him and wipe his feces. Perhaps he was teaching me that in order to be a master you first must serve.

The gallstones required emergency surgery. He refused to go to the hospital, and I had to sling him over my shoulder and carry him to the doctor on my back. When I brought him to hospital, he berated me endlessly.

"Seeds For Hell! You are always trying to kill me!"

He called me into his room before I left to study in Taiwan. There were red packets on the table, the kind we use in Asia for monetary gifts.

"Whatever is here is my blessing to you," he said. "Whatever is here is yours."

When I opened the packets and counted up the money it was enough for a ticket to Taiwan, one way. To this day I think that he sifted through the packets and took out all the larger bills. There was no kindness in him. He made me feel like an adopted child. That is the Chinese way.

He trained me to be mindful and exact. In retrospect, I see that he prepared me for Korea.

I learned from him never to say, "I don't know how."

"Seeds For Hell! You have time to say you don't know how. Why don't you take that time to go learn?"

Sometimes I'd make him angry on purpose, in a kind of passive-aggressive display of pique or to make him angry for my own amusement. After I cleaned the table, I would place his cup in a slightly different place than where I had found it. As a calligrapher, he was incredibly exact, and the lack of precision I displayed infuriated him. "The cup goes here, not there," he would hiss, moving it a centimeter one way or another. "I'm not going to teach you. I'll let you be taught by your disciples."

My mantra was earliest-latest, most-least, first-last. I woke up earliest and went to bed latest, did the most and ate the least. I was the first to take the blame and the last to get credit.

Song Nian was fond of repeating the parable of the waving flag.

Two monks were looking at a flag blowing in the wind and arguing. One said the flag was moving; the other said it was the wind that was moving. Wind or flag? They went to their master to settle the issue. "Neither flag nor wind," their master said. "The mind is moving."

Song Nian rarely smiled but recounting this little story invariably seemed to amuse him.

In the morning service if I hit the wooden fish, singing bowl, gong, or drum wrong, he would peer around, looking under things and making a great display after we were done.

"What are you doing, master?" I would ask.

"Looking for the lost notes. Have you seen them?"

He scolded me with poems.

I used my true heart
To face the moon.
Who knew
The moon was facing a drain?

"Drain" in this case could be thought of as toilet or sewer.

I was his last disciple. It seems I am always the last disciple. Maybe in my past life I was naughty. That is why it has always been my karma to be taught by dying men.

It is important to be able to take hardship, and basic to Chan is the concept that nothing precious and to be cherished is easily obtained. A bit of pressure is good. It's healthy. Pain is an inevitable part of growth, and pain is necessary for spiritual development.

We have a traditional saying: "If the disciple, no matter how you scold, will not run away, then you go to the next stage." You chase him away. No matter how you try to chase him, if he doesn't run away, then you go to the third stage. You beat him. If he still doesn't run away, only then do you begin to teach him.

Before I left to go to Taiwan, Song Nian blessed me from his wheelchair. I didn't want to leave him; I didn't want to go away. He was saying mantras and making *mudras* and murmuring to himself. He placed both his hands on my head and intoned: "The alms bowl for a thousand families. The lonely, wandering monk will travel ten thousand miles. I'll see you in a week," he said. I thought he must have lost his mind. Aside from the gallstones, he'd had two strokes and several major heart attacks. He refused to take heart medicine. His cardiologist, a younger man, died before him. He was a tough old bird.

I bid him farewell and flew to Taiwan. Three days later I got the news that he had died. It took me four days to arrange my ticket. I was back in Singapore exactly seven days later. The president and prime minister of Singapore attended his funeral. It took me seven years to build a *stupa* for his ashes.

When I was in Taiwan after he died, I would ring the big bronze bell after the evening service before the monastery closed up for the night. The bell was at the top of a hill in the main hall. It was over two meters high, forged in Taiwan. The ringer was a ram of wood that was slung on ropes. You rang the bell 108 times in the morning to wake everyone up and 108 times in the evening.

I'd chant verses between rings. One went:

Children who run away from their families
Lonely travelers
Wandering in distant lands
May they return home soon
And be reunited
With their loved ones

When I sang these verses, my heart went out to everyone wandering, everyone like me who was far from home. The rich tone of the bell reverberated over the hills in the coming dark. I thought of Song Nian's blessing. I never guessed that one day I would be back at his monastery and take over as abbot. That is where I am now.

I didn't want to return, but people were saying Song Nian was unlucky because he didn't have any disciples. His monastery would be closed and fall to ruins, and he would soon be forgotten. It would be as if he had never lived. So I felt I had to return. What can I say? I'm Chinese. And this too is part of the character and spirit of Chan.

Acknowledgements

There are always people, after my retreats, who ask me if I have a book. My reply in the past has always been no! Until now.

This book began when I went to Indonesia in 2007 to teach and then returned there in 2008, 2009, and 2010 to lead retreats.

My Indonesian students were very sincere, earnest, and gentle. They asked me about a book in 2010, and I told them it was too much trouble and I was too busy to think about it. Some time after the retreat, I received an e-mail. It seemed that a group of six volunteers had transcribed all my talks—240 single-spaced pages (I guess I talked a lot). I was moved to tears by this gesture and it filled me with joy.

The transcription was done under the direction of Agus Santoso in Jogjakarta, who I first met in my teacher Sheng Yen's retreat center in Pine Bush, New York. Agus suggested I contact Kenneth Wapner, who had developed and edited

Master Sheng Yen's autobiography in English, *Footprints in the Snow*, to see if Kenneth thought the transcripts could be turned into a book. That is how *Essential Chan Buddhism* was born. Things come about when you least expect them.

This book is dedicated to all those who helped in Indonesia. Brothers Buntario and Selamat Tigris have been the force behind building the wonderful Sheng Yen Center in the lovely, forested hills outside Jakarta.

My deep thanks also go to Djemi Lim, Wiratna Sari Wiguna, Johanes Sungarda, Yuliana Yang, Eric Hermanto, and Hanley Tarsat. Without them there would be no book. Their dedication and initial belief in the project made it possible.

My thanks also go to the Ekayana Buddhist Center in Jakarta, who first invited me for a teaching tour and Bhante Aryamaitri and Bhante Dharmavimala.

I would also like to thank Paul Cohen of Monkfish Book Publishing for bringing *Essential Chan Buddhism* to Western readers. I know Master Sheng Yen would be pleased.

I could continue writing and thanking, but I'd better stop. Peace to all.

Guo Jun Fashi
Sheng Yen Center, Indonesia
2011

ABOUT THE AUTHOR

CHAN MASTER GUO JUN was ordained as a novice monk at Mahabodhi Monastery, Singapore, under Venerable Master Song Nian and received his full monastic ordination at Guangde Monastery, Taiwan, under Venerable Master Jingxin, Venerable Master Liaozhong, and Venerable Master Guangyuan.

Dharma heir of Venerable Master Sheng Yen from Dharma Drum Mountain, Taiwan, and Venerable Master Qinyin from Fuhui Monastery, Taiwan, Venerable Guo Jun is the lineage holder and successor of the Chan (禅), Xianshou (贤首), and Cien (慈恩) schools of Chinese Buddhism. He has also studied and practiced in Thai, Burmese, Chinese Pure Land, Tibetan, Korean Son, and Japanese Shingon traditions.

Guo Jun was the deputy director of Dharma propagation at Singapore Buddhist Federation and abbot of Dharma Drum Retreat Center in Pine Bush, New York. He is a member of Australian Psychological Society; spiritual and guiding teacher of Chan Meditation Centre Australia, Chan Community Canada, and Dharmajala Indonesia; and abbot of Mahabodhi Monastery, Singapore.

Guo Jun has a diploma in biotechnology from Ngee Ann Polytechnic, Singapore; a degree in Buddhist philosophy from Fuyan Buddhist Institute, Taiwan; and a bachelor of arts in psychology and sociology from Monash University, Australia. He graduated with a master's degree in Buddhist studies at the University of Sydney, Australia.

Guo Jun is actively propagating the teachings and practices of Chinese Buddhism. He has taught in different parts of the world such as Australia, Canada, Europe, Indonesia, North America, and Singapore.